"Howard Rasheed has written an important and timely book! I highly recommend this book to anyone seeking an integrated framework for utilizing innovation best practices."
—*Dr. Robert DeFillippi author and Director of the Center for Innovation and Change Leadership, Suffolk University*

"This timely and valuable book is going to be a winner!"
—*Tom Looney, former Industry Director, Microsoft, and Founder, NextChannel Partners*

"Dr. Rasheed demonstrates a keen understanding of what it takes to spark innovation."
—*Dr. Miles Davis, Dean of the Byrd School of Business, Shenandoah University*

"This must-read book should be part of your business library as it will strengthen your position in the marketplace."
—*Janice Laureen, Executive Director, The Association for Strategic Planning*

"This book is a must read for global organizations who want to remain competitive through innovation."
—*Dr. Dwayne Jakes, The Start up Business Coach*

INNOVATION STRATEGY

Seven Keys to Creative Leadership and a Sustainable Business Model

HOWARD RASHEED, PH.D.

iUniverse, Inc.
Bloomington

Innovation Strategy
Seven Keys to Creative Leadership and a Sustainable Business Model

iUniverse books may be ordered through booksellers or by contacting:

iUniverse
1663 Liberty Drive
Bloomington, IN 47403
www.iuniverse.com
1-800-Authors (1-800-288-4677)

ISBN: 978-1-4697-8044-3 (sc)
ISBN: 978-1-4697-8045-0 (ebk)

Library of Congress Control Number: 2012903388

Printed in the United States of America

iUniverse rev. date: 04/30/2012

CONTENTS

Part I: Strategies for Creative Leadership

ACKNOWLEDGEMENTS

Foremost, Praise and Glory to the Creator of Heavens and Earth, my Benefactor and Guardian.

To my lovely wife Linda, who encourages and supports me in all my efforts to make a difference.

To my children Candace, Derick, Hassan, and Mikal, who serve as my inspiration to set an example.

And to my 7 grandchildren who remind me of the importance of leaving a legacy of positive change for the world they will inherit.

Thanks also to Michael Roney and Michael Utvich of High Point Publishers for development editing and my wife Linda for her proofreading.

PREFACE

THE SKY IS FALLING:
WHERE IS THE "RESET" BUTTON?

During the height of the economic crisis each day I went to my business strategy class at the University of North Carolina Wilmington and started my lecture by putting a "big number" with a dollar sign on the board for my millennial audience. Each number, bigger each day, indicated how deep we were sinking into an economic chasm and each day the line at the "corporate bailout ATM" was growing longer.

As the weeks progressed, my students' smirks of arrogant disbelief turned to widened eyes of hopelessness, and I found myself becoming apologetic on behalf of the baby boomers that have squandered our dominance in the world. Our lack of proactive response to a hyper-competitive global economy has endangered the future standard of living for the coming generations and the anticipated comforts of our golden years.

As the red ink and staggering deficits mounted daily, my seniors, who were days from launching their careers, stared back in frustration. They were starting to realize that the world they were promised had come pre-mortgaged.

"So 'Doc', now that we are thoroughly depressed, do you have any solutions?" they asked me with an undertone of sarcasm.

In response I paraphrased Thomas Friedman's conclusion in the final chapter of *The World is Flat*: "Innovate or die!"[1]

"Ok, cool, let's get started," they replied with eager naivety.

Unfortunately, this was easier said than done.

"Remember those 'big numbers' I have been putting up on the board for the past two months?" I asked them. "None of those include investments in new technology, infrastructure or re-training our future knowledge workers. That $10 trillion in debt you will be paying for with your first real paycheck, if you get a job, is just to pay for our generation's consumer habits and our inability to maintain our economic advantages inherited from the 'greatest generation' after World War II."

"So how do we retain our economic standing in the world?" my students asked.

"First we establish innovation as a national priority on the level of homeland security and energy self-sufficiency," I replied. "We need a Kennedy-like, man on the moon, national innovation imperative. Creating an innovation based economic agenda at the national level which can trickle down to stimulate a regional innovation economic development strategy."

To illustrate that concept, I shared with my class some of the work my company, the Institute for Innovation was doing in Brazil. My work with the Center for Strategic Studies (CGEE), an NGO sponsored by the Ministry of Science and Technology involved preparing a strategic plan for 34 sectors of their growing economy. We devised a collaborative innovation approach to build a national and local value network. The objective was to anticipate technology disruption and develop plans to proactively discover new technologies, markets and process improvements.

I explained to my students that I had not only been working with the Brazilian R&D technologists, but also with that country's economists, regulatory administrators, and social scientists in order to facilitate a collaborative, open and ongoing innovation process.

Utilizing this strategy, not only does the U.S. government have to invest in infrastructure, but it also must serve as catalyst for research using federal funding in the value network. Academic institutions then will be able to leverage this investment to commercialize technology and facilitate new venture development. Of course, it will require business incubators, a viable venture capital network and a globally competitive workforce with world-class education and skills.

As I explained all of this, the students' eyes glazed over, and then reflected a glimmer of hope. "Gosh, at least somebody has a plan," someone offered.

"That's right folks, but remember, I was talking about Brazil, not the U.S. We have been told we can't afford that kind of investment, even though the reality is that we can't afford not to."

The students just stared at me for a second or two. Then someone called out, "Hey Doc, where is the "reset" button?"

Are You Ready to Lead an Innovation Renaissance?

What is needed globally is a renaissance in creative leadership and innovation that results in growth and prosperity for organizations and citizens around the world. Using innovation methodology developed by the Institute for Innovation, this book provides ideas and tools that will make you and your organization more successful. Whether your organization is a Fortune-level global brand, an international non-government organization (NGO), a government intelligence agency or a solo professional practice, you can be successful and win the future using the concepts of innovation in this book. It gives you a roadmap for becoming an **Innovation Strategist** who can lead an "innovation renaissance" in your organization.

So what exactly is a renaissance?

- A revival in the world of art and learning
- A renewal of life, vigor, interest, and attention
- A provocation: something that incites, instigates, angers, or irritates
- A rebirth: a renewed existence, activity, or growth of interest in the creation of new ideas.

An innovation renaissance is a renewal of new ideas that create value—nationally, organizationally, and individually. It is not only essential for the world economy and the nation, but also for you as a leader in a competitive world. It will transform your organizational fortunes, as well as our collective future.

As with the Agricultural and Industrial Revolutions, we are in the midst of a major paradigm shift in the way the world is run. Some have called it the "new knowledge economy." Whereas land and capital were traditionally the key elements of production, knowledge and intellectual capital will be the primary currencies of the future.

We need to embrace this concept now. At the end of the first millennium, medieval Europe was transformed by the infusion of philosophy, literature, and scientific discovery from Asia and Africa. Similarly, we should expect a major transformation of the new global economy based on the discovery of new knowledge and its conversion into value for economic and social benefit.

One of the basic tenets of the Renaissance period was Renaissance Humanism, which assumed that it was possible to develop human potential through more universal learning. Knowledge was not restricted to practical professions or science, but also to subjects like rhetoric, history, and philosophy—the *humanities*—and people were empowered with limitless capacity for development. As such, the gifted citizens of the Renaissance embraced many disciplines of knowledge and developed capabilities in many subjects. When someone is referred to as a "Renaissance Man" or "Renaissance Woman" today, it suggests a broad and profound knowledge of many subjects and the proficiency or the accomplishments of an expert.

Innovation Strategy provides seven transformational strategies that will help you develop creative leadership skills. These strategies represent a unique approach to innovation that will inspire you to become a "renaissance" person in your own industry, organization, or competitive arena. I call this new role **The Innovation Strategist**. I believe that innovation skills can be taught and one can accelerate innovation by utilizing a replicable and sustainable system.

Of course every book or consultant claims to have the magic formula for success. I wrote this book because the research at the Institute for Innovation over the past eight years indicates our methodologies and systems are unique, effective, and make a significant contribution to innovation strategy.

What Makes This Book Different?

Many books are filled with generalities, anecdotes, and platitudes from the "cold case files", but fail to provide specific systems and tools to make a business model replicable and sustainable. Despite all of the efforts by other authors, what has been missing from the idea marketplace is a replicable and holistic system to face innovation challenges of the 21st century. *Innovation Strategy* provides a theoretical framework and concrete examples for a system that can be implemented in any organization.

There are several other tomes that take an editorial tack similar to this book. They tend to focus on technology and product innovation, particularly breakthrough, radical or disruptive innovation. For example, David Crossner's *Innovate the Future*[2] addresses technology innovation, particularly in the information technology sector. A very popular series of books from Clayton Christensen, including *The Innovator's Solution*[3], *The Innovator's Dilemma*[4], and *Seeing What's Next*[5], focus on disruptive product innovation—products such as the iPod, which dominate their market niches and change lifestyle patterns forever.

One key distinction is that *Innovation Strategy* focuses on **business model innovation**. It provides an actionable innovation system with the potential to yield significantly enhanced, more reliable results for your organization and the overall economy. Breakthrough product innovation "grand slams" certainly are exciting, creating new markets with the potential mega-returns associated with "first mover" and sustainable competitive advantages; however, swinging for the fences also increases the likelihood of striking out.

Extending innovation to your business model increases the likelihood of creating value at all functions and levels of the organization. Business

Model Innovation is available to any organization, regardless of size, product, or the extent of their R&D budget.

A recent survey conducted by IBM, titled "What Executives Really Want," indicates that businesses are now directing more attention toward disrupting existing business models.[6] It found that CEOs who select creativity as a leading competency for their employees are far more likely to pursue innovation through business model change. In keeping with their view of accelerating complexity, they are breaking with traditional strategic planning cycles in favor of continuous, rapid-fire shifts and adjustments to their business models.

The highly regarded book, Business Model Generation[7] by Alexander Osterwalder, provides a very creative framework for business model architecture. Another title, *Seizing the White Space*[8] by Mark Johnson (one of Christensen's co-authors), actually focuses on business model innovation, providing a four-box model for finding innovation opportunities and case studies that illustrate the author's white space metaphor of how companies found opportunities outside its core. In *Innovation Strategy*, I expand on Osterwalder and Johnson's frameworks with a more comprehensive approach to business model innovation. Using an ecosystem metaphor, I describe the continual renewal and refinement of the business model as the core strategic transformation initiative of an organization. Unlike any other title on the market, this book not only provides a framework for a business model and examples of innovation from the past, but also offers a systematic guide for leading an innovation renaissance in your organization that is holistic, proactive, and sustainable. Using this **Sustainable Innovation Ecosystem** you can create your own competitive future.

Connecting the Dots

What is unique about this Sustainable Innovation Ecosystem is that it is built on the premise that creative intelligence leads to innovation and can be stimulated and institutionalized. To stimulate creative intelligence we extend the popular systems thinking metaphor referred to as "**connecting the dots.**" Of course "dots" represent knowledge or information. Our innovation system goes beyond the typical divergent and convergent thinking models to help you systematically "**connect the dots from different boxes**." This multi-dimensional thinking process as illustrated in Figure 0-1 can produce more interesting opportunities for discovery.

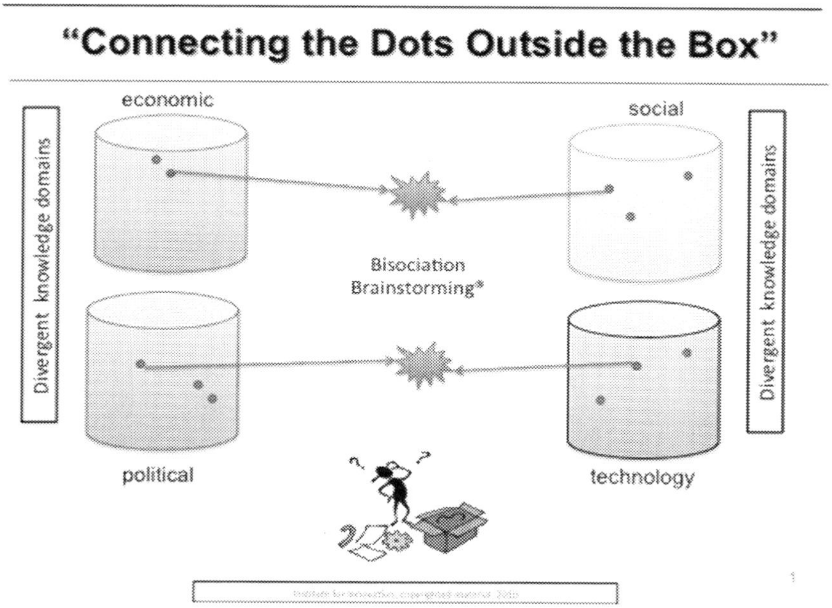

Figure 0-2: Connecting the dots from different boxes stimulates knowledge creation and discovery.

This system for connecting the dots is a proprietary business method developed by the Institute for Innovation called **Bisociation Brainstorming®.** Based on recent neuroscience research this process helps you focus attention on the many permutations of converging trends and emerging issues from multiple knowledge domains to discover new opportunities and innovative ideas. In other words, it is not just a knowledge management or sharing system it is a knowledge creation system. By creating a replicable system innovation can be institutionalized.

Inside the Book

Part One of *Innovation Strategy* discusses three of the seven keys **Creative Leadership**. The introduction makes the case that we are living in increasingly disruptive times. Our new global economic imperative is—**Innovate or Perish**! In the future, economies will be faced with new uncertainties. New technology will be fraught with risks, and markets will continue to change rapidly. Value networks—the interactions between an organization's value chain and its external stakeholders—will be subject to hyper-competitive disruption. Being reactive to the certain disruptions caused by your global competitors will result in certain failure to sustain a competitive advantage.

In Chapter 1 the first key suggests that creative leaders must **Anticipate a Future of Disruption**. Depending on what you and your organization value you will experience shifts in your value curve. These shifts are tipping points that could indicate pending disruption in your strategic environment.

Chapter 2 suggests that creative leaders must **Intentionally Create Disruption** as part of a proactive innovation strategy that is responsive to global competitive challenges. This disruption must go beyond technological innovation from R&D and apply to all strategic transformation efforts of your organization. The **Triangle of Innovation** concept presented in this chapter demonstrates how to target your creative disruption efforts and accelerate opportunity recognition in strategic foresight, product development, and strategic planning activities.

Chapter 3 explains how to **Inspire Creative Intelligence** of your stakeholders as the core element of developing creative leadership and an innovative culture. Systematically stimulating ideation rather than just managing and sharing knowledge can be the differentiator for a healthy and vibrant innovative culture. Practical tools for assessing the innovation style of your stakeholders will help maximize interactions and diversity of thought that supports the co-evolution of your stakeholders in a productive innovation ecosystem.

Part Two of *Innovation Strategy* addresses the final four keys for **Sustainable Innovation**. Chapter 4 provides a step-by-step guide to **Business Model Innovation** that will help you convert disruption into opportunities for growth and prosperity. I use the ecosystem metaphor to illustrate how to cultivate the interdependent components of the business model. Recent United States patent law changes provide interesting opportunities to use business method patents to improve the sustainability of your reinvented business model. The templates provided include a comprehensive list and description of emerging business models that can be applied to efforts to reinvent your business model. A series of audit questions will provide a systematic inquiry process for analyzing each element of your business model. "Call to Action" exercises throughout the book serve as an experiential blue print for business model innovation engagements in your organization.

Chapter 5 entitled **Cultivate an Innovation Ecosystem,** describes the Institute for Innovation's **Six Step Collective Intelligence System**™. It is a systematic approach to innovation that provides Innovation Strategists with tools to visualize their strategic environment, explore new knowledge, discover new opportunities, innovate new ideas, envision new futures, and measure the effectiveness of innovation initiatives.

Chapter 6 discusses how to **Engage with Collaborative Technology**. Collaborative innovation networks and technologies are the great enabler of internal and external stakeholder engagement. Additionally the **Idea Accelerator**™, an electronic brainstorming system created by the Institute for Innovation is a complement to our Six Step Collective Intelligence system. It provides a practical application for overcoming the traditional limitations of group collaboration. This state-of-the-art Innovation 2.0 software connects your thought leader and stakeholder networks globally to stimulate and capture the potential avalanche of ideas that will result from your innovation efforts.

Chapter 7 explains how to use this system to **Make Innovation Viral** to ensure your stakeholders embrace the alignment of innovation culture, systems, and technology. Overcoming organizational inertia is a real challenge for institutionalizing innovation and making it a consistent part of your strategic transformation efforts. This strategy utilizes social networking and social media techniques to build the social capital necessary to make sure your initiatives easily adopted by your stakeholders and maximize your return on investments in innovation.

Part III addresses how the Innovation Strategist can "**Win the Future**". It provides best practices from the Public, Commercial, and Social Sectors supported by case studies that include global perspectives in Strategic Foresight, Technology Commercialization, and Strategic Planning. Chapter 8 describes **Best Practice in Strategic Foresight** using engagements done on behalf of the Ministry of Science and Technology in Brazil that were documented in an article entitled *Discovering The Next Big Idea*.[9] Chapter 9, **Best Practices in the Commercial Sector** illustrates new product development using a case study of technology transfer at a university. Chapter 10, **Disruption in the Social Sector,** addresses social transformation using an example from the disruption along the Gulf Coast of the United States caused by the British Petroleum oil spill and the disaster of Hurricane Katrina.

The concluding chapter shows how the Institute for Innovation is using the principles in **Innovation Strategy** to build their future competiveness. We use the convergence of four major trends—business analytics, mobile computing, social media, and cloud computing—to design a sustainable business model for the future.

Develop New Skills as an Innovation Strategist

What knowledge or skills do you need as an entrepreneur, executive, or thought leader to proactively embrace the innovation imperative? To become a creative leader and develop a sustainable business model you must adopt the mentality of an Innovation Strategist and apply these concepts to whatever field or level of the organization you are responsible for leading. As an Innovation Strategist you will need to:

- Understand the competitive dynamics of your industry and society.
- Anticipate future disruptions, scenarios, and paradigm shifts.
- Reduce risk and uncertainty in your environment.

- Rethink future possibilities that can be opportunities for innovation.

Using the ideas in this book you will learn how to:

- Implement a proactive innovation strategy of **Creative Disruption** for your industry and organization.
- Create an innovation culture that empowers stakeholders with **Creative Intelligence.**
- Establish a **Sustainable Innovation Ecosystem** in your organization.
- Use **Collaborative Innovation Technology** to engage your fellow innovation stakeholders.
- Identify business opportunities for entrepreneurial investment and venture creation.
- Identify opportunities for new products, markets, and technology applications.
- Design plans for the future of national and regional economies, industries, and organizations.
- Utilize tools for testing the viability of ideas for value creation and innovation projects.

As you accept the urgency of an innovation imperative for "winning the future," I hope this book serves as a thought-provoking and useful guide to finding your innovative solutions. It is intended to be a source of inspiration and practical strategies for you to become a change agent in government, the commercial sector, or the social sector. By using this book as a guide you can provide solutions that can transform enterprises and transform lives around the world.

The bottom line: We need an innovation renaissance, and we need it now! Let's begin the journey.

INTRODUCTION

INNOVATE OR PERISH!

"If a man does not know to what port he is steering, no wind is favourable to him."

—*Seneca, Roman dramatist, philosopher, & politician (5 BC-65 AD)*

The New Global Imperative

The beginning of the new millennium's first decade was marked with turmoil and the end was defined by chaos. So begins an era of disruption. The recent global recession should be a wake-up call to the fragility of an economy built on a weak foundation of financial manipulation, rampant consumerism, and excessive debt.

There have been many previous warning signs of the dangers of excessive speculation and unfettered capitalism. In the United States there was the financial disruption of the savings and loan scandals in the 1990, when over-inflated real estate values led to collapsing investment portfolios and prison terms for executives convicted of fraud. The largest was the Lincoln Savings and Loan collapse in 1989 that cost the United States federal government $3 billion. Nearly 23,000 bondholders were defrauded and Charles H. Keating, Jr., the Chairman, served four and a half years in prison.

1

At the end of the 20th Century the creation of the Internet and the web browser ushered in a new brand of global capitalism. In just a few short years, the dot-com crash caused a major economic disruption. The landscape became littered with failures on a grand scale.

Take Pets.com, for example. They burned through millions of dollars on memorable Super Bowl advertisement. But even with the support of Amazon, they could not turn an $82.5 million initial public offering into a viable brand and subsequently closed in nine months. Another example, Fooz.com, was based on a $35 million bet that people will use want to use something other than credit or regular currency for trade. Even the stardom of Whoopi Goldberg could not save it.

Adding to the avalanche of economic failure from the bursting of the Internet bubble there were other major disruptions. War on two fronts in Asia by the NATO alliance after 9/11 and the war on terrorism were major paradigm shifts in perceptions of security and safety. The dissolution of the Soviet Union and the entrance of China into the World Trade Organization changed the global economic landscape by adding formidable competitors into global capitalism.

But… we hit the snooze button, again, and went into a sleep so deep that the next alarm caused us to jump out of bed and hit our heads. As we lay stunned for what seemed an eternity, our lives of endless prosperity flashed before our eyes like a distant dream. We awoke to a new reality that the snooze button was no longer available. We would actually have to get up, get dressed, get to work and be productive. How in the world would we do this?

As we staggered from the "Great Recession," an additional reality set in. Nearly five years after the natural disasters of Hurricane Katrina and Rita, one of the biggest man-made natural disasters occurred. On the same day it celebrated the technological milestone of the deepest well in history, the Deepwater Horizon rig exploded in the Gulf of Mexico off Louisiana in April 2010, killing 11 workers and spewing more than 200 million gallons of oil from an undersea well owned by BP. In the weeks that followed we experienced an onslaught of destruction, economic chaos, and ecological ruin. The spill soiled sensitive tidal estuaries and beaches, killing wildlife and shutting off vast areas of the Gulf to commercial fishing.

After seeing a *60 Minutes* account of the human error that compounded a technological failure on the ill-fated oilrig, it struck me: *This is an innovation challenge of the highest magnitude!* Innovations in deep-water oil drilling technology have taken us to this point, but innovation has not risen to the level to solve the challenge we now face.

It is ironic that only months before the Deep Water Horizon disaster, the ban on deep sea drilling was lifted. At the time, this made sense to all except the environmental hard-liners. The policy change was embraced by the vocal chorus from the conservative side of the U.S. Congress to "drill, baby, drill." It seemed like a relatively safe alternative to nuclear energy or the continued political and economic consequences of our growing energy addiction to foreign oil—not to mention the potential conflict that could result from the insatiable need for energy by other global powers like China.

This disaster reminded us of the ecological implications of our unbridled pursuit of fossil fuel beneath the ocean. Despite the warnings of global warming and the security risks associated with our dependency on foreign sources of fossil fuel, we still have not quite gotten the message. To win the future we must create new alternative, renewable, and clean energy sources or we will suffer the consequences.

But have we learned our lessons? Although BP settled their court case in early 2012 to the tune of $7.8 billion, the company reported profits of $40 billion, $7.7 billion alone in the last quarter. It recently raised its dividend to shareholders by 14 percent. BP recently said it has 5 deep-water rigs operating in the Gulf of Mexico and expects to be operating an additional three by the end of 2012. Our memories are short and our global need for energy continues to increase. Evidently we still have lessons to learn to win the future in energy.

Howard Rasheed, Ph.D.

The Urgency of Winning the Future

The next decade of this new millennium began with organizations desperately looking for the "new normal." The recent economic crisis shattered traditional business paradigms. Dynamic changes in the global economy, technological advances, and the evolution in consumer and market demands have put great competitive pressures on businesses and organizations throughout the world. New economic realities suggest that competition in the emerging knowledge economy has become more complex while the pace of change has accelerated dramatically.

Economic systems are universally experiencing a paradigm shift in which knowledge resources such as information, human capital, and intellectual property are more critical than land, natural resources, and labor. The manipulation of knowledge resources affords new sources of wealth creation based upon innovative intellectual assets, collaborative learning networks, and the effective infusion of advanced technology.

Discovering and mastering new knowledge that captures these complexities and keeps pace with hyper-competitive change has become an important competence for creating value. Institutionalizing innovation and creativity within an organizational knowledge network in order to stimulate awareness and learning may be the most important organizational competency of the future. In fact, it's essential for creating and sustaining competitive advantages in the new global economy.

Institutionalizing Innovation and Creativity

Considering the potential value of the "next big idea," leaving innovation to random and serendipitous flashes of brilliance is not a proactive approach befitting industry leaders. To be ready for the innovation renaissance, you must learn how to institutionalize innovation by first accepting the following premises:

- There is a global competitive imperative to innovate or perish.
- Innovation is the core competence of sustainable competitive advantage.

4

- Innovation and creativity do not have to be serendipitous and left to the chance of random occurrences of inspiration by a lone inventor.

Innovation and creativity can be institutionalized as a systematic and replicable process to catalyze an organization's strategic transformation process. This book will help you as a creative leader to cultivate a sustainable innovation system in your organization so you can perpetually reassess and reinvent your business model. This approach is particularly important in light of the recent economic downturn and challenging road ahead. A continuous process of refining your business model is the new frontier of value creation. Fortune-level companies and emerging entrepreneurial firms alike are finding that they can get a better return on their investment by focusing on realigning their business model rather than high-risk R&D.

The seven innovation strategies I outline in this book form a roadmap that will enable the stakeholders in your organization to become creative leaders of innovation, and is based on the following key conclusions:

- An innovation system can be sustainable if it provides a replicable and institutionalized process for discovering opportunities to intentionally create disruptions in your value network. New ideas are created not just from product development, but also from value creation in strategic foresight and strategic planning activities to perpetually reinvent your business model. The business model then becomes the strategic guide to effective new venture development, organizational change and business processes.
- A strategic ecosystem provides an enlightening organic metaphor for aligning the important external elements of an organization—environment and knowledge—with its internal elements—people, system and technology.
- Creative disruption is a paradigm shift in innovation that is a more proactive and science-based system that will accelerate the pace of value creation.
- Organizations that do not innovate will perish!

Innovation: The New Core Competence

A ground swell of consensus has developed for the idea that sustainable innovation is becoming an important new core competence for organizations and the key to global comparative advantage and regional economic prosperity. This has become apparent to some of the more iconic CEOs. For example:

- William Ford Jr., chairman and CEO of Ford Motor Co., recently announced that "innovation will be the compass by which the company sets its direction" and that Ford "will adopt innovation as its core business strategy going forward."
- Jeffrey Immelt, chairman and CEO of General Electric Co., has talked about the "innovation imperative," a belief that innovation is central to the success of a company and the only reason to invest in its future.
- Steve Ballmer, Microsoft Corp.'s CEO, stated recently "innovation is the only way that Microsoft can keep customers happy and competitors at bay."

Business leaders are also recognizing that innovation requires creative leadership. According to a new survey conducted by IBM's Institute for Business Value of 1,500 chief executives, "creativity" was identified as the most important leadership competency for the future success of an organization.[10] That's creativity—not operational effectiveness, influence, or even dedication. Coming out of the worst economic downturn in their professional lifetimes, when managerial discipline and rigor ruled the day, this indicates a remarkable shift in attitude.

This also is consistent with the study's other major finding: Global complexity is the foremost issue confronting these CEOs and their enterprises. The chief executives see a large gap between the level of complexity coming at them and their confidence that their enterprises are equipped to deal with it. Until now, creativity has generally been viewed as fuel for the engines of research or product development, not an essential leadership skill that must permeate an enterprise.

If innovation needs to be institutionalized creativity must become a core competence that can be taught or transferred as human, intellectual or social capital. Some would suggest that creativity can't be taught. I agree that some people are more naturally prone to be creative. But I also believe that our education system strips creativity starting in kindergarten in order to achieve order through conformity. In a survey conducted by the Institute for Innovation 75% of futurists and business leaders agree that creativity can be stimulated. The problem is, most (66%) reported they do not have a replicable innovation system.

If every human has imagination, I believe we can provide processes and tools to systematically stimulate creativity in humans that can result in innovation. This concept is at the heart of a global *innovation renaissance*. Let's start with an American perspective on this innovation imperative.

Comparative Advantage in Decline: An American Perspective

Decades of rampant complacency, unrealistic living standards, and unproductive financial manipulations have put America on the brink of losing its dominant position in the world economy. America needs an innovation renaissance to renew our comparative advantages in the global economy.

Comparative advantage as defined by Michael Porter[11] refers to the ability of a person or a country to produce a particular good or service at a lower marginal cost and opportunity cost than another person or country. This theory of comparative advantage has been an enduring benchmark of global competitiveness.

Although innovation is being increasingly cited as the salvation for the United States' global competitiveness, some alarming trends are revealing a decline in our contribution of innovative products to the global marketplace compared to some other nations. It's true that between 1990 and 2003, high-tech products positively contributed $243 million to the U.S. balance of trade, while all other goods resulted in a negative cumulative total of $3.4 billion. The U.S. global share of high- tech industrial output declined from 31 percent in 1980 to 18 percent in 2001.

Discourse from government and corporate thought leaders usually convey a vague aspiration toward maintaining our advantage in innovation, but it lacks substantive solutions. The Task Force on the Future of American Innovation, which issued *"The Knowledge Economy: Is the United States Losing Its Competitive Edge? Benchmarks of Our Innovation Future,"* predicted the following trends in global innovation that are already having a prominent impact on the comparative advantage of the U.S.: [12]

- U.S federal spending on R&D as a percent of GDP is declining
- China and S. Korea are increasing R&D spending
- The U.S. has declined to 11th in basic research as a percent of GDP, as of 2010
- U.S. companies are moving R&D offshore
- U.S. venture deals in India & China are dramatically increasing
- The U.S. high-tech trade deficit is dramatically increasing
- Analysts predict that 90 percent of scientists & engineers will live in Asia in the next decade
- It was estimated that 52 percent of engineering jobs and 31 percent of finance jobs could be outsourced in the coming years.

According to the report:

> The United States still leads the world in research and discovery, but our advantage is rapidly eroding, and our global competitors may soon overtake us. It is essential that we act now; otherwise our global leadership will dwindle, and the talent pool required to support our high-tech economy will evaporate…this is not just a question of economic progress. Not only do our economy and quality of life depend critically on a vibrant research and development (R&D) enterprise, but so too do our national and homeland security.

If we look at the value created by innovative products in America and remove entertainment and adjust for piracy, we have a much more realistic, yet pessimistic picture. American scientists are losing ground in terms of the percentage of academic articles being published globally, as well as the number of patents being filed.

Another alarming trend related to our innovation competitiveness is that the U.S. is losing ground in science, technology, engineering, and math (STEM) education according to the following statistics from the Congressional hearings: [13]

- In 2009, China graduated 219,600 engineers, representing 39 percent of all the Bachelor's degrees in that country.
- The U.S., in that same year, graduated only 59,500 engineers, or five percent of all the Bachelor's degrees.
- Furthermore, 58 percent of all degrees awarded in China during 2009 were in physical sciences and engineering, compared to 17 percent in the U.S., a figure that is dropping by about 1 percent a year.
- Of the U.S. science and technology workforce, 38 percent of the Ph.Ds. were foreign born in the year 2000. At the same time, China is producing far more tech-savvy workers than is the U.S. (650,000 a year in China versus 220,000 in the U.S.). India, meanwhile, produces 95,000 graduates a year in electrical, information technology, and computer-science engineering—the kind in highest demand—while the U.S. turns out 85,000 a year.

Outsourcing Innovation: The Loss of Creative Intelligence

The most serious threat to comparative advantage is the loss of creative intelligence, which is the ability to create new solutions, ideas, and technologies. With the U.S. outsourcing more and more creative high-tech and engineering positions to other countries, we face a brain drain of the ability to apply our collective intellect to creative means that advance our society.

As demand climbs for engineering skills, any company that relies on engineers will have to fill part of that demand in Asia. In fact, a Booz Allen Hamilton (BAH) and India's National Association of Software and Service Companies (NASSCOM), study estimated that as many as six million engineers are available in emerging markets to take on R&D assignments of all sorts, with 28 percent in India and 11 percent in China. The study found that the worldwide outsourcing of innovation is growing far more rapidly to nations such as India, China, Thailand, and Brazil than in the U.S. This shift is different from the non-engineering information technology, manufacturing, and business processes that have been outsourced and offshored, since innovation is even more important to the company's attempts to sustain a competitive advantage.

The Booz Allen/NASSCOM study also indicated that:

- Current global spending on offshored engineering is $15 billion. By 2020, the figure will expand to $150 billion to $225 billion, with the growth coming from emerging markets such as India, China, and Russia.
- Reduced labor costs account for more than 90 percent of offshored innovation work in emerging markets today.
- In the next 10 years this trend will be driven by strategic priorities: market access, resource quality, increased productivity, and expanded capacity.

We are witnessing the early stages of a revolution in innovation services. Another report from Booz Allen Hamilton indicates that a major shift is occurring away from the conventional wisdom that smart companies don't outsource the core operations that define them and set them apart from the competition[14]. Now, it seems to be quite the opposite: companies are increasingly contracting out elements of their engineering, design, and research and development. Technology and engineering expertise is shifting to Asia, Eastern Europe, and even Africa.

According to the BAH report, some respondents are moving R&D operations to key local markets, such as China and India. Consequently, the offshoring of high-skill high-technology work is increasing, with even research moving offshore. For example:

- Accenture's CEO expects that the company will soon have more workers in India than any other country, including the U.S.
- IBM was projected to have 100,000 workers in India by 2010, more than one-quarter of its workforce, rivaling the U.S. as the leading country for workers.

According to testimony before the United States Congress[15], China, India and other developing countries have governmental policies to actively attract innovation jobs and work. For example, the Chinese government often requires technology transfer as a condition on investments in China by multinational corporations, and India offers tax holidays for any exports from its information technology services industry.

These hearings also included testimony of firms investing in plants and R&D facilities in low-cost countries. Companies like General Electric, Eli Lilly, Google, and Microsoft are expanding R&D centers in India and China, which will work on cutting edge research and new product development rivaling their centers in the U.S. In fact, a University of Texas study found that of the 57 recent major announcements of locations of global telecom R&D facilities in the past year, more than 60 percent were located in Asia, whereas, a meager nine percent were located in the U.S.

The conclusions reached in the Congressional testimony include the following:

- It is crucial for the U.S. to remain the incubator of new business ideas and the first mover when it comes to providing new goods and services. If we are to remain big exporters as the rest of the world advances, we must specialize in the sunrise industries, not the sunset ones.
- As the world's leading nation, the U.S. must grab the first-mover advantage in a disproportionate share of these. And that, in turn, requires that we remain a hotbed of business creativity and innovation. To accomplish this, basic research, industrial R&D, creative and aggressive business management, an entrepreneurial culture, an active venture capital industry, and the like must all remain integral parts of the American success story.
- Nonetheless, there are a number of vital roles for the federal government in such areas as fostering basic science and R&D, supporting scientific and engineering education, returning both the tax code and the budget to sanity, maintaining competition and open trade, and keeping the capital markets vibrant but honest.

Howard Rasheed, Ph.D.

Federal Policy: Falling Short

The U.S. has made policy decisions that don't fully support a broad view of innovation. For example, these policies offer subsidies and grants for R&D, but not for state-of-the-art information technology for logistics and supply chain management, such as those innovated by Wal-Mart. Tax credits for capital equipment and for brick-and-mortar structures should be expanded to these types of enterprise resource planning systems.

Additionally, policymakers have offered investment tax credits to buy computer hardware or software, but not for the cost of training users, adapting hardware and software systems to the specific needs of a company, or reengineering its business processes to accommodate them.

Why is this important? The global revenues generated by technology activity in the U.S. accounted for nearly half of the $72 billion services surplus in 2004. Typically, U.S and foreign-based multinational companies draw on the technological base they have developed through R&D and business development here in the U.S. and use it in operations throughout the world. To lose this advantage would significantly add to a growing trade deficit.

The major point is this: *The United States appears to have a dramatically receding edge in innovation.* Since the advent of a global economy, the world has "flattened," to use Thomas Friedman's metaphor.[16] America benefited from the evolution of the Internet, but that invention then became the great equalizer in terms of creating economic value. American organizations used to be able to take advantage of being inventors and first movers in the markets they created. But those waiting for the good old days of American (or even Western) domination to return will be in for rude awakening. Americans can't count on our historical dominance in innovation to maintain our position as the leading superpower. In fact, too often the organization that invents a disruptive technology does not reap the long-term benefits. And too often the beneficiaries of disruptive technologies are in other emerging economies.

An effort to address this imperative is represented by The National Innovation Act. In an effort to accelerate innovation in the United States, The Act would:

- Raise funding for basic research and math & science education at the National Science Foundation (NSF) and National Institute of Standards and Technology (NIST)
- Encourage multidisciplinary learning and research
- Require a study on how the federal government should grow the high-value service economy through research, education and training
- Establish a mechanism to sustain, assess and coordinate the nation's innovation policies
- Coordinate federal economic development programs to support collaborative innovation in regional innovation hotspots

Innovation Economics: Turning Smart Ideas Into Growth

Innovation economics has emerged as a fundamental concept as Americans search for an answer to its declining dominance in the global economy. In a recent *Business Week* cover story, author Michael Mandel suggests that innovation economics show "how smart ideas can turn into jobs and growth and keep the U.S. competitive." The underlying assumption is that products, services and business models can create growth and economic prosperity. The article refers to several historical approaches (primarily prizes, government spending, and tax credits) as economic development strategies.[17]

According to this article, financial investments have not yielded significant returns based on measurements such as employment in technology based industries. Self-proclaimed innovation economists are now studying the lack of innovation return on investment, as well as research and development initiatives, to understand successful innovation models in an effort to turn smart ideas into jobs.

In his book *Innovation Nation*[18], innovation guru John Kao discusses the pros and cons of commonly used concepts such as incubators and innovation clusters. Unfortunately, proximity, the cornerstone of geographic economic development policy, has been rendered less important due to Internet-based outsourcing, global talent sources, and global venture capital networks. Consequently the global availability of resources has contributed to pockets of innovation sprouting all over the world.

But there is a paradox that serves as a barrier to traditional economic development models. The concept of multi-factor productivity suggests that technological change and business process improvements accounted for 45 percent of productivity between 1987 and 2007.[19] The problem is that the primary measure of successful economic development has been employment growth, which is counteracted by productivity improvements. Still, innovation ranks as the most important factor for long term growth by 95 percent of economists as reported in the *Business Week* article. But recent failure in industries with high growth expectations such as biotechnology and nanotechnology has been a source of disappointment.

Mandel makes the point that open innovation models are based on business or technical problem solving by the collaborative efforts of diverse stakeholders and technologists. At the same time, he recommends outsourcing R&D as a way to remain competitive. An additional risk to outsourcing is the loss of high-end knowledge workers. This approach to economic development can't be very appealing to an area with world-class research institutions such as in the Research Triangle area. This risk is not limited to shifts from one region of the U.S. to another. Now regional innovation excellence can move to any area of the world with quality education, political stability and strategic incentives.

To remain globally competitive leaders must develop a viable innovation economics model that must be considered from a value network perspective. A value network is an organization's ecosystem that includes its supply chain and its external stakeholders. In other words, innovation cannot continue to happen in a vacuum by lone inventors using research inconsistent with stated strategic objectives. Instead, a model built on the concept of a value network that facilitates open, distributed, and collaborative innovation should provide the platform for linking all stakeholders in a regional economic ecosystem. The stakeholder and public policy initiatives must include focused federal sponsored research, academic institutions, venture capital networks, virtual business incubation, and regional planning agencies. Small business development agencies, for technical support and global trade assistance, should support this innovation ecosystem. A tax system should provide incentives for strengthening the value networks including the development of a world-class workforce and infrastructure, while maintaining an excellent quality of life and standard of living for the citizens.

There are some well-founded concerns that there is a problem with implementing a national innovation agenda on a regional basis. Specifically, there are challenges related to defining the regional system's domain, implementing functional regions and securing sufficient regional knowledge infrastructure. Regional economic plans are sometimes incapable of coping with the structural problems connected to innovation and globalization. Part of the innovation renaissance must address the realities that innovation economics is a global issue.

The Innovation Challenge

Some say that necessity is the mother of invention. It can also be said that invention is the mother of innovation. The purpose of innovation is to create value, whether economic, or for improving the quality of life. When early humans needed light, they discovered fire. When they needed to move objects, they invented the lever. When they needed to defend themselves against animals, they fashioned weapons. When they needed to work more effectively, they invented tools. After humans create and invent, they then find additional value in the invention by sharing it with others in exchange for some mutual benefit.

The innovation challenge has been a story of survival. When threatened by external forces with superior weapons, social groups either invented better weapons or were vanquished. When a competitor creates a superior product, organizations create value or lose market share and/or profit. *The story remains the same: Innovate or perish!*

One lesson from the British Petroleum Deepwater Horizon oil spill disaster is that we must find clean, renewable, and available sources of energy or our quality of life and our security may be in jeopardy. I can think of no other innovation that will have the same level of global impact on creating value. And value comes not only in the forms of economic profit and wealth, but also as security and improved quality of life from a sustainable environment. Our innovation challenge is to either find the next big thing that will create this value, or suffer the consequences.

But this book is about more than the challenge to find better sources of energy or focus on the "next big thing" in technology innovation. Leaders from all sectors need to innovate from many perspectives. There is a strong need among C-suite executives such as operating and planning officers, chief innovation and knowledge officers, entrepreneurs, and executives of new and high-growth ventures to answer the endless challenge of innovation when confronted with many ongoing questions such as:

- How can we maintain a sustainable competitive advantage?
- What is the next big thing in our industry?
- How can we increase wealth?
- How can we achieve profitable growth?

Leaders in the public sector are also faced with questions of great importance. Leadership at the federal, as well as state and local officials, should ask:

- How can we improve the quality of life in society?
- How can we increase the safety and security of citizens?
- How can we protect our environment?

As you can see from this short list of questions, it is necessary to expand the concept of the innovation challenge beyond inventing a disruptive technology, a new product, or new service. What are the innovation challenges you may face as leaders, managers, or ordinary citizens concerned about the future of our planet?

Commercial Sector Challenges

There are many challenges that we face as leaders, depending on whether we operate in the public or commercial sector. For example, some of the macro-level challenges faced by commercial sector leaders are to:

- Understand changing environmental dynamics
- Improve ability to adapt and respond to changing conditions
- Anticipate future possibilities: opportunities and challenges
- Reduce risk and uncertainty
- Create sustainable competitive advantage
- Improve the global competitiveness of your organization
- Create sustainable economic value
- Create shareholders wealth
- Increase return on investment

At a more micro perspective, leaders are continuously challenged to:

- Increase revenue sources
- Improve quality and performance
- Reduce costs
- Improve efficiencies
- Create new knowledge
- Share existing knowledge and information
- Improve organizational competencies and capabilities

The never-ending challenges of an entrepreneur include the need to:

- Identify potential investment opportunities
- Develop strategic alliances and partnerships
- Create new products and services
- Commercialize technologies
- Anticipate new market applications for existing technology

I purposely put technology-based innovation at the bottom of the list to emphasize the point that the innovation challenge is very broad and therefore needs a new perspective.

Public Sector Challenges

To further broaden this perspective, you can look at a long list of innovation challenges leaders in the Federal level of the public sector face:

- Improve nation's comparative advantage and trade accounts
- Reduce national deficits and debt
- Improve government efficiency
- Improve access to information and services for citizens
- Improve technology transfer from the public sector to the commercial sector
- Find sustainable energy sources
- Protect the quality of the physical environment
- Reduce energy consumption
- Anticipate and neutralize security threats

Organizations in the public sector are faced with unique innovation challenges for the benefit of society. As government deficits mount at the state and local levels, leaders must find innovative ways to address some the following issues:

- Improve quality of life
- Improve standard of living
- Improve regional competitiveness
- Improve access to and quality of consumer goods
- Improve workforce skills
- Improve the quality of education
- Improve safety of citizens
- Provide and improve transportation for citizens
- Provide for clean and healthy environment
- Increase opportunities for employment
- Improve the quality of entertainment and recreation

Social Sector Challenges

In the social sector, organizations have a mission to address the needs of the disadvantaged and under-served segments of society. Leaders in this area must create sustainable social value to address needs that include:

- Inequities in social justice
- Lack of access to affordable health care
- Achievement gaps in education
- Access to affordable housing

- Inequities in access to jobs and workforce preparation

In an environment with significant funding gaps from government sources, leaders in the social sector must find innovative ways to:

- Identify sustainable revenue sources
- Develop opportunities in public-private partnerships
- Develop opportunities from government privatization trends

What Keeps You Up at Night?

I am sure you found something on the previous lists that keeps you up at night. What is high on your own priority list of issues and concerns? We must recognize that all sectors in our economy and society need innovation that is focused on creating value beyond disruptive technology. How can high-performance organizations in all sectors address these challenges through innovation? They must:

- Be relentlessly outcome and value-focused
- Be highly efficient
- Be aware of changes in their environments and able to translate insight into action
- Be highly focused on their core capabilities, and adopt outsourcing strategies to improve efficiencies in non-core activities
- Take a hard look at what services actually need to be delivered and consider who is best placed to provide those services
- Identify more effective and efficient delivery models
- Identify the best solution for service delivery—whether internal, external or mixed economy
- Face unprecedented demand to make significant cost savings while potentially having to deliver more in terms of quantity and quality of services to customers.
- Take a radical approach to deal with the "more for less" imperative, which may need a fundamental challenge to existing arrangements
- Identify alternative ways to do business and deliver successful customer, community and partner outcomes

The Innovation Solution: A Competitive Renaissance

The diversity of human intellect and its ability to create may soon be humankind's last competitive advantage over the microprocessor-based machine. Harvesting this capacity and challenging this unlimited human potential should yield immeasurable possibilities for the future. As expressed in the universal law popularized by *Star Trek*'s Dr. Spock: "From infinite diversity comes infinite combinations." This challenge continues today. From the many unexplored galaxies within this vast universe there are systems of knowledge that defy the grasp of human intellect.

But if accessing the infinite possibilities of ideas that can emerge from the efficient application of human intellect is so important, leaving it to the unsystematic randomness that is characteristic of art seems to be an inefficient means of creating intellectual capital. Organizations invest billions of dollars in systems to research and develop new products and processes, acquire new markets, and deliver new products or services. If that is so, why are there so few systems for new knowledge and idea creation?

The basic definition of innovation is the creation and conversion of ideas into viable commercial products, in addition to building a foundation for future sustainable growth. In this context it is knowledge, not capital, that is the core component of innovation. Emergent idea creation that creates new knowledge is an important function in organizations for stimulating innovation.

The Innovation Ecosystem: A Renaissance Metaphor

The inspiration for *Innovation Strategy* is rooted in the divine laws of nature. A renaissance is a renewal process, much like we see in an ecosystem. Using the lessons we learn from the Creation, I illustrate a metaphor of an innovation ecosystem, called the *Sustainable Innovation Ecosystem* (SIE), to explain how to create an effective strategy and nurture a sustainable innovation culture.

In nature, an ecosystem is an environmental system of interacting and interdependent relationships of organisms, bound by natural resources and the flow of energy from soil, air, sunlight, and water. Like an ecosystem, the global economy is a complex system of relationships between economic and human entities. In nature, inequalities and imbalances are caused by natural disasters, such as tsunamis, drought, and tornadoes, but there are also man-made imbalances caused by war, oppression, and corruption.

Likewise, the global economic ecosystem is fraught with change and uncertainty that will cause disruptions or opportunity. We need a sustainable "innovation ecosystem" that can address the needs of a new global economic reality. I use the natural ecosystem metaphor to illustrate the point that a truly sustainable innovation system for winning the future requires an organic approach to learning. It will illustrate the need for a holistic innovation system—a guide for Innovative Strategists armed with new paradigms that will cultivate a future of growth and prosperity.

The renewable aspect of a Sustainable Innovation Ecosystem is evident in the creative disruption seen in the dynamic laws of nature. A classic example is the evolution of the seasons and the growth of plants. The natural progression is that ripened fruit is harvested, and un-harvested fruit falls to the ground where seeds germinate for another cycle of growth. In this cycle of life, we see that the plant does not have to die or be destroyed to evolve to next level of growth or to yield value each season. Vegetation can renew each season with the proper amount of sunlight, water, and fertilization to yield fruit. With appropriate nurturing of the innovation ecosystem this process should be sustainable.

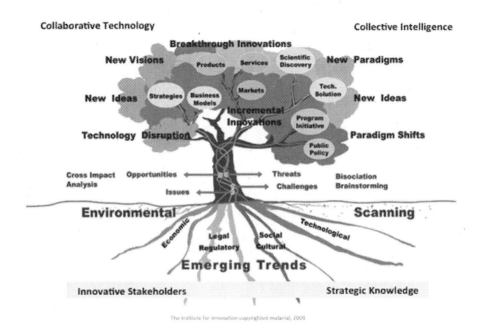

Figure 0-1: The Sustainable Innovation Ecosystem explains how to create an effective strategy and nurture an innovation culture.

The renewing energy of innovation comes from the continuous flow of knowledge fueling an emergent system of complex interconnections. These dynamic interactions can produce infinite possibilities for growth and harvesting the fruit of the most viable solutions. This ecosystem perspective takes into account the complex interdependencies that exist in the environment at all levels, from micro to global. As such, innovation systems can be considered as complex, dynamic, and emergent systems of multi-functional and multilevel interactions of activities and resources.

The Sustainable Innovation Ecosystem metaphor illustrates how complex systems and patterns arise out of a multiplicity of relatively simple interactions. The Sustainable Innovation Ecosystem diagram provides a view of this emergent ecosystem. In the innovation ecosystem, the four main elements are:

1. Strategic Knowledge
2. Innovative Stakeholders
3. Collective Intelligence System
4. Collaborative Technology.

Strategic Knowledge is the starting point of the ecosystem. The emergent characteristics of the innovation ecosystem refer to the complex interactions of diverse sources of knowledge. Aligning stakeholders, system, and technology is covered in Part 2 of this book.

New Strategic Knowledge: Ecosystem Energy

Any vibrant environment needs energy for growth. In the Sustainable Innovation Ecosystem (SIE), the critical energy source is knowledge. An innovation renaissance is dependent on knowledge creation and discovery. In our SIE, this rebirth and revival starts with strategic knowledge that is extracted from the information rich environment (soil). Successful innovation depends upon a (root) system of knowledge discovery that feeds information from diverse sources. The environmental scanning process extracts knowledge from the macro environment that is typically categorized as technological, political/regulatory, social/cultural, and economic.

The creation of new knowledge serves as the energy source for recognizing and exploiting opportunities. The SIE perpetually uses new knowledge to stimulate innovative minds, in a nurturing environment with efficient tools, to produce ideas that can be harvested for value-creating activities. The degree, to which knowledge is created, diffused, and absorbed is the key determinant of the vitality of growth and development.

Historically, knowledge has been defined as a tacit quality that resides in the minds of individuals, while explicit knowledge is articulated, codified and stored in organizational media. These definitions only depict static information in dormant environments. In reality, knowledge systems are a dynamic and complex interaction of informational units within an environmental context.

Three basic issues are critical to the quality of the energizing the SIE:

1. How the knowledge energy passes through the semi-permeable organizational boundaries. This is determined to some degree according to how the communication of knowledge and technology passes between organization entities, which is enabled further by creating contact points that are multifaceted.
2. The degree to which the flow of knowledge is from moving between dynamic and static sources.
3. The degree to which knowledge is absorbed through the root system, which refers to how organizations learn and discover new knowledge that may help them to create value.

Transcend Complexity

Knowledge does not exist as isolated bits of data, but from a complex, dynamic, and holistic system of independent, yet inter-related and infinite intersections of information. This characteristic of the knowledge system is analogous to the co-evolution concept of the ecosystem, where organisms depend on other organisms based on their position in the food chain. As the knowledge passes through the root system, analyzing the interaction of this dynamic information results in the recognition or discovery of opportunities and threats in the environment. Successfully discovering and anticipating these future possibilities will result in new ideas (fruit). These new ideas can come in the form of new scientific discovery, new products or services, new strategies, new business models, new programs, and new policy initiatives. These ideas could be technological disruptions that range from breakthrough to incremental or major paradigm shifts in the way we think and our basic assumptions.

To transcend complexity at the organizational level, we can use the value network analysis as a holistic view of your environment and its complex interdependencies. This view focuses on the emergent and dynamic system of multi-functional and multilevel interactions of activities and resources. This value network perspective helps managers find opportunities to add value through interactions with customers, suppliers, complementary vendors, intermediaries and other external stakeholders. Government and industry leaders can take a broader view of their value network for proactive economic development and industrial sector competitiveness.

Transcending complexity requires a more scientific approach to innovation that systematically makes sense of knowledge and permutations of knowledge interactions in complex environments. From this deliberate approach to dynamic knowledge, we can recognize opportunities that can effectively be transformed into value added ideas and technology. Most existing knowledge systems manage, store, and disseminate information, but fail to provide a replicable methodology that stimulates human cognition for new idea creation and opportunity recognition. A true system of innovation not only allows it to be replicated in diverse industries and applied to problematic challenges, but it also stimulates creative potential in more diverse sectors of society and varied hierarchies within the organization. This book is an opportunity to share the knowledge that will accelerate this renewal process with you, the new Innovation Strategist.

Get Ready to Lead the Innovation Renaissance

To lead the innovation renaissance the Innovation Strategist must become a systems thinker. Systems thinking is the understanding how things influence one another within a whole. In the ecosystems metaphor of nature, system thinking involves understanding how air, water, movement, plants and animals interdependently interact to survive or perish. The innovation ecosystem consists of people, structures and processes that work together to make an organization vibrant.

As the Innovation Strategist, you are the organizer and enabler of the ecosystem that can make your organization more innovative. Just as biological processes such as radiant absorption and photosynthesis cause systematic growth, we need to understand and transform the disruption and apparent chaos of your environments into opportunity. A sustainable innovation strategy is the process needed for abundant prosperity in your strategic environment.

In Part I this book presents strategies for creative leadership, starting with a proactive approach to anticipating disruption and an organic innovation strategy called creative disruption. It also presents the concept of creative intelligence that provides a scientific based mental framework for creativity. This methodology can inspire creative leadership, create an innovative culture, and build innovative systems that are holistic and sustainable.

PART I

Strategies for Creative Leadership

CHAPTER 1

ANTICIPATE A FUTURE OF DISRUPTION: KEY #1

The basic law of the jungle: You are the hunter or you are dinner.

Disruption—The Mother of Innovation

In business, you can either be the disrupter or be disrupted. But one thing is for sure: disruption is an eventuality. It is just a matter of when, who, how and whether you thrive or survive. Successful entrepreneurs are typically disrupters. They find customers who have needs, understand how those needs represent an opportunity rather than a challenge, and create a product or service that customers value sufficiently to generate above average returns on investment.

The first key to being a creative leader and becoming a catalyst for the innovation renaissance is to adopt a proactive approach to anticipating disruptions in the future. Because of the fast pace of a hypercompetitive global economy, this process must be continually renewed, refined and reinvented. Without a strategy for innovation, successful entrepreneurs eventually lose their competitive advantage and fall into a competitive chasm. You must continually ask yourself:

Have you *anticipated* the major disruptions that will affect our global economy?

Are you *ready* for the next wave of disruption?

The future is full of potential disruption. The current state represents the static condition of status quo. But status quo is a misnomer because your environment is constantly experiencing change, risk, uncertainty and competition. Thinking that there is a status quo is a false assumption of those who are not paying attention to their environment. There are constant changes in the strategic environment in the form of disruptive technology, disruptive economies, disruptive markets and disruptive networks.

There are disruptions that affect the macro economy, commercial sectors and industries. For example, the attack on the World Trade Center on September 11th created a major disruption in the Western economy. Hundreds of billions of dollars have been spent globally since then on the war on terror. The attack has affected our national and state budgets in terms of the costs for security. It has affected the way we travel. It has led to racial and religious distrust. The two wars in Iraq and Afghanistan have resulted in thousands of lives lost, both military and civilian. The potential disruption caused by preemptive military intervention to prevent Iran from developing a nuclear weapon could have consequences far beyond the flow of oil through the Gulf of Hormuz.

A History of Disruption

History is full of examples of social, political, economic and technological disruptions. Many civilizations have grown to the status of world domination and have then experienced some disruptive event or convergence of events that resulted in their decline. Some of these civilizations are depicted in Figure 1-1. Some predict that China will be the largest economy based on GDP between 2030 and 2040.

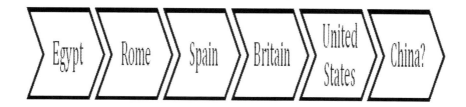

Figure 1-1: There has been a continuum of civilization disruptions.

At each break in the continuum of civilization there was some kind of disruption, such as war, regime change, epidemic disease or fleets lost at sea. Major shifts in power are often associated with a technological breakthrough in the prosecution of war. The invention of gunpowder, canons, repeating rifles, radar and atomic bombs each had a major effect on the balance of power and the dominance of an empire. Wars have had deciding battles as their tipping points. Napoleon had Waterloo, the Civil War had Gettysburg, and the Allies in World War II had Normandy and Hiroshima.

A typical disrupter associated with war was the failure to protect the empire because it extended beyond its logistical capacity to support military success. For example, Rome began to collapse after its military did not have the financial incentives of the captured treasures (war booty) of vanquished foes. After successfully expelling the Moors, the Spaniards set sail to discover the "New World" and created value from seizing precious resources. This exploration opened the window of opportunity for the slave trade going west and precious commodity imports on the trip back east. But the Spanish Empire eventually collapsed from trying to maintain its conquered empire over vast distances.

After the defeat of the Spanish Armada, the British Empire benefited from opening trade routes to the east, benefitting from opium trade in China and slave trade to the western hemisphere. At one point it was said, "the sun never set" on the British Empire because it extended around most of the planet. The British and Dutch East Indian companies were the forerunner of the modern stock-based multinational corporation who dominated commerce with the support of their respective nations. The British were also the forerunners of the illegal drug cartels with their government-sanctioned trade in opium resulting in a third of the Chinese population as users at the height of the Second Opium War.

As for the United States, its global economic dominance developed because it was able to control the indigenous population for free land and collaborate with Europe in the slave trade for free labor. The major disrupter benefiting the U.S. in modern history was the victory in Europe and Japan at the end of World War II. This left the U.S. as the only major world power with infrastructure that was not devastated by war.

In terms of the socialization of society, the United States has gone through a number of cycles of disruption to include colonization, slavery, territorial expansion, segregation, mass immigration, and diversity. At some point, the early settlers were content to be British subjects, but somewhere along the way taxation without representation initiated a rebellion that led to the American Revolution. The issue of slavery fueled the debate for state's rights which led to the Civil War. The major disruption for segregation was the Civil Rights movement. Political debate still rages about porous borders and the globalization of labor.

Disruptions have also characterized the evolution of products within many different industries. As shown in the Figure 1-2, technology disruptions have changed the standards and dominant platforms in the music, movie media, television, and communication media industries. In each industry example, can you predict "the next big thing"?

Music

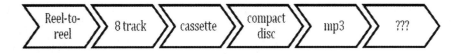

Movie Media

Television

Print Media

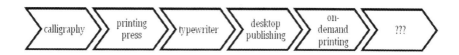

Figure 1-2: Disruptions abound throughout the media industry.

As you can begin to see, disruptions abound throughout the media industry in general. Many major city newspapers have failed since more people started getting their news from major network TV and the Internet. During the first Gulf War, the appetite for 24/7 visual news coverage gave a disruptive boost to the fledging cable news station CNN. As the Internet boomed in the late 1990s, more independent sources of news and information became available.

I recently saw an interview of professional journalists who lamented that the standard verification of information sources may become a thing of the past as people turn to unverified and questionable sources for information. Traditional print media are often torn between traditional delivery systems and the demand for more timely and accessible sources—which can mean changing their business model to an Internet delivery system. Their business dilemma question: should they cannibalize their print publication by embracing the Internet, or run the risk of becoming irrelevant? At risk is their ability to monetize their advertising revenue stream if they don't devise a new financial model.

The media industry isn't the only sector where disruption plays a key role, as shown in Figure 1-3. In retail, disruption has had a major effect on how we shop. The mom-and-pop corner grocery stores were supplanted by franchises that moved to strip malls to survive. Major downtown department stores with lunch counters moved to regional malls with food courts. Globalization resulted in discount stores that evolved into superstores.

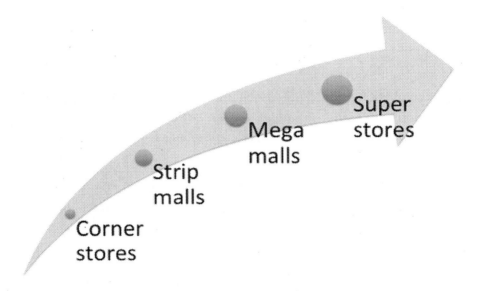

Figure 1-3: The disruptive evolution of retail outlets.

Now, even superstores have seen their days. "Big box" stores such as Best Buy have begun sub-leasing part of their floor space. They also have announced plans to double the number of smaller format Best Buy Mobile Stores that focus on smartphones and tablets, two high trending product lines. Other large retailers such as Staples, Wal-Mart and Office Depot are also thinking smaller for their future locations.[20]

Making Sense of Chaos

Anticipating disruption requires that you are comfortable making sense of what appears to be a chaotic new world order. An Innovation Strategist sees disruption, not as random chaos in complex global markets, but as opportunity to create value that is unique. If you were able to predict how the Internet has enabled the rise of Facebook and the fall of Blockbuster you probably do not need to read this book. *If you did not, then continue reading.*

A recent Fast Company article coined a new phrase, GenFlux, to describe, "a mind-set that embraces instability, that tolerates—and even enjoys—recalibrating careers, business models and assumption."[21] This new breed of entrepreneurs and executives will possess the skills to interpret and thrive in chaos.

There have been a number of great disruptions that will continue to influence who will win the future. The Innovation Strategist who uses this book will be prepared to join the GenFlux generation to anticipate this future of disruption, make sense of apparent chaos, and lead the innovation renaissance.

The Internet: The Great Disrupter

Industries are being created and destroyed faster than ever. The Internet has played the role of the great disrupter as new products are developed, technologies are commercialized, and new business models emerge. New technology platforms such as the MP3 have left old CD and tape technologies in the dust. More importantly, this technology disruption has given birth to paradigm shifts in the way we listen to music, share music, and access music through business model innovations like iTunes. Upcoming technologies in the media industry will fundamentally change standards, delivery mechanisms, and our paradigms for visual perceptions.

Consider the global cell phone business. Five years ago Nokia, Research in Motion, and Motorola controlled 64% of the smartphone market. Now Samsung and Apple dominate the market. Were you able to predict the surge of startups with valuations of over $200 million such as Airbnb, Dropbox, Flipboard, Foursquare, Gilt Groupe, Living Social, Rovio and Spotify? These companies have come out of nowhere with business model innovations that have capitalized on the technology disruption caused by the Internet.

The Internet will continue to be a major disrupter and source of business model innovation as it is expected to grow by 1300%, create several million jobs, and reach over 6 billion users in the next few years. You can expect that technology will accelerate the disruption in your business model as your competitors develop better value, new markets, improved infrastructure and new financial models. eBay and Google are examples of new business models based on creating value from software algorithms that provide services that did not exist before. eBay created a consumer-to-consumer intermediary platform by using the Internet. Google became a verb for using a search engine in everyday vernacular.

There will also be disruption in your value network as primary and secondary processes change and relationships with external stakeholders evolve. More of the primary functions in the large corporations in Western economies are being outsourced. This started more than 20 years ago, with manufacturing facilities being shifted offshore. It has now evolved to sending service jobs overseas as well, to places such as customer service centers. We are also outsourcing secondary functions in information technology, accounting and R&D functions, primarily because of the disruptive force of the Internet.

The key response to this uncertainty is to be proactive and intentionally create disruption. This will ensure that the future state of your environment is what you want it to be. Even General Electric, one of the few Fortune 100 holdovers from the Industrial Economy, is changing the way it responds to disruption. They have begun to hold their top 650 managers accountable for more focus on external stakeholders, how to get and apply external knowledge, how to lead ambiguous situations, and how to improve on collaboration.[22]

For large companies as well as small, flexibility to adapt to or organize the chaos will require an Innovation Strategist who can anticipate disruption. Thriving in disruption will also require skills to manage changing relationships between internal and external stakeholders in the Value Network using collaborative innovation systems and tools.

Economic Globalization: A Future of Disruption

Some would argue that the future of disruption in our new economy will be determined by economic globalization, which is "the global distribution of the production of goods and services, through reduction of barriers to international trade such as tariffs, export fees, and import quotas, and the reduction of restrictions on the movement of capital and on investment".[23]

Globalization has enabled China to become a major exporter and build up massive foreign exchange reserves. The $3.2 trillion in their sovereign wealth fund has typically invested in government bonds, particularly in the United States. Now that the credit rating for the U.S. has gone down in 2011 for the first time in history, the Chinese are changing their investment strategy. Now they are investing in emerging markets in the financial sector, mining, power, and infrastructure in markets such as Poland. Coincidently, the year 2011 marks the 100th anniversary of the Chinese revolution of 1911 and what is considered the start of modern China.

As 2012 begins major European countries such as Italy, Greece, and Spain face credit default. The ratings agency Standard & Poor's downgraded the government debt of France, Austria, Italy and Spain on January 13th. The downgrades are jeopardizing the Eurozone's ability to overcome a worsening debt crisis. All together S&P cut its ratings on nine Eurozone countries, including Italy, Spain, Portugal, and Cyprus. S&P also cut ratings on Malta, Slovakia and Slovenia. If we are in a symbiotic global economy, the big question is: What do these disruptions mean for Western capitalism?

One of the most critical disruptions that have had a major impact on the shifting fortunes in the global economy is *outsourcing*. There is a seminal economic theory called **factor price equalization** that explains the rise and fall of economic fortunes in globalization due to outsourcing. Basically it states that the factors of production will move to the country or region with the lowest costs. This assumes that the other factors of production such as materials and workforce skills are sufficiently similar in terms of cost, access, and quality. As the targeted region prospers, average wages increase and consequently the cost of production increases until another region's cost structure becomes competitive. At some point manufacturing shifts to the least cost area and the cycle starts again.

The automobile industry shifting from the U.S. to Japan and then to South Korea is an example of this economic phenomenon. Manufacturing outsourcing is now shifting to China. The difference between China and Japan is size of population. It will take a lot longer for the average wages of such a populous country to increase to the point it is no longer competitive. Add to this point, the fact that China is still a hybrid of capitalism and communism. This allows the Chinese government to control factors such as the value of currency as well as provide government subsidies and rapid mobilization of resources in targeted areas such as the Apple manufacturing facilities in Foxconn City. But there are indications that factor price equalization is starting to take effect on the Chinese offshoring phenomena.

Based on a 2011 report by the Boston Consulting Group there is a new trend developing called "reshoring" which is the reverse of offshoring. As labor and shipping costs are increasing in China some industries are finding it makes economic sense to move some or all of their operations back to the United States. In the last ten years labor costs in China have increased over 500% from $.58 to nearly $3 USD from 2001 to 2010. Currently Chinese wages are rising 15 to 20% while the labor supply is drying up. In general, this trend could result in an increase in 2 to 3 million jobs and adding $20 billion to $55 billion in output annually to the U.S. economy[24].

The furniture industry, which has suffered in my home state of North Carolina, is one of the seven industries reaching a tipping point in reshoring because the cost of shipping bulky products is increasing due to rising fuel costs and because there is an ample supply of domestic wood. Also delivery times from China can be as long as three months compared to one month for furniture produced in the US.

Social media has become a major tool of disruption by enabling uprisings in the Arab world. My recent visit to Cairo and a walk through Tahrir Square was a reminder of how disruptions can result in revolutions. Discussions with executives, taxi drivers, and a former Egyptian Cabinet Minister suggest there is a great deal of uncertainty, but a tremendous amount of hope for the ability of the country to reinvent itself for the modern global economy. The former Minister was proud of the fact that Egypt is fourth in international call centers, but recognized the need for infrastructure that supports an innovative culture. For example, it takes tens of thousands of equivalent US dollars and several months just to get a business license without paying bribes. Civil laws for property, contracts, and intellectual property laws are still not conducive to a business culture.

This is consistent with a report about economic development in Tunisia after they served as a catalyst for the Arab Spring. The report, "Tunisia: from revolutions to institutions,"[25] was sponsored by infoDev, a global technology and innovation program at the World Bank Group and conducted by consultants from Reboot. The report suggests that technology-oriented small and medium-sized companies (SMEs) can generate economic expansion and job growth in Tunisia because of Arabic and French language skills and lower labor costs. However, the cost of doing business, government control of critical markets, and the lack of a market-responsive higher education system that produces better skilled workers are major growth impediments.

Protests for Occupy Wall Street and similar demonstrations have been organized on Facebook, real-time visuals of civil unrest have been sourced on YouTube, and all of this reporting has been supplemented on Twitter. Facebook was even used to make Bank of America retract its plans to charge fees for debit cards. Technology and social media are a major source of political as well as economic disruption.

Green Energy: The Next Big Disrupter

The next big disruption is likely to be in the area of green energy or low-carbon emission innovations. This is particularly true for energy used in the manufacture, delivery, and consumption of goods and services. In a recent report by the Pew Foundation, "The Business of Innovating: Bringing Low-Carbon Solutions to Market"[26] the following was predicted:

1. Global energy consumption is expected to grow by 40 percent in the next two decades.
2. The replacement value of the aging global energy supply infrastructure is estimated to be $12 trillion.
3. Global revenues from new low-carbon energy solutions, energy efficiency technologies and services, and other climate-related businesses are projected to surpass $2 trillion by 2020.
4. Between 2010 and 2020, the projected cumulative total investment in clean energy generation alone is expected to reach $2.3 trillion.

The report concluded that early disrupters that anticipate and capitalize on the emerging opportunity for green energy innovations will influence emerging policies and standards, as well as, achieve higher market share through product leadership.

According to the report the keys to success in fostering green innovation are:

*   Managing policy uncertainties in innovation strategies
*   Clear direction and commitment from leaders
*   User-focused value propositions
*   Business model innovations
*   Nexus policy—organizing networks of stakeholders to allow innovation to take hold
*   Robust innovation strategies
*   Partnerships, investments and acquisitions

As organizations respond to the opportunities to replace existing energy sources they will create new technologies and business models that will disrupt the value presented by the existing product life cycles of incumbent firms. Predicting value curves for innovation life cycles of new products and services will be an important skill for the Innovation Strategist to develop.

Disruptive Value Curves

Human activity is inherently focused on creating value from disruptive activities. But value is a very generic term that means different things to different people or organizations. Throughout this book I will refer to stakeholder value to describe a broad concept of how value creation applies to all members of your value network. It could be economic value, or something more abstract, such as intrinsic value.

Economic value creation is the *raison d'etre* in business. Public entities create value in more abstract terms, such as quality of life, safety and liberty. Social entities are concerned with justice and inequities. Some well-being values have been quantified in terms of standard of living, literacy and consumer confidence indices.

What about the individual? However you define it or measure it, your value changes over time. This cycle of change can be represented in a value curve. From a personal perspective, your economic value can be measured in terms of:

- Disposable income
- Net worth
- Standard of living
- Credit score

There are a number of personal disruptive forces that can change your value curve, such as your employment status or extraordinary expenses from a major illness. Maybe you expected a disruption like college tuition, but the scholarship you hoped for did not materialize. Likewise, you may know your parents are aging, but you never know when a slip and fall will accelerate the process.

For example, your economic value as represented in Figure 1-4 could be measured in terms of disposable income and net worth. A disruption to your personal value curve could occur when you are laid off from work or a major illness occurs. Your disposable income goes to zero and you have to dip into your savings to make up the deficit, thus your net worth declines as well. Later your your disposable income recovers, but the damage to your net worth has not been restored. These values change over time, as represented by the value curve below:

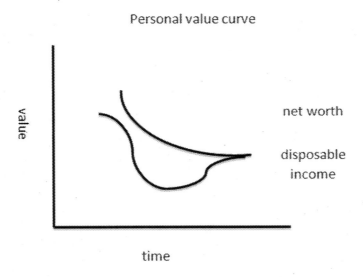

Figure 1-4: Your personal value curve fluctuates over time.

A business value curve could be measured in terms of:

- Gross revenue
- Market share
- Net profit
- Market capitalization

As we know, change is the only constant. A major disrupter such as the recent financial crisis has a significant impact on consumer spending and gross revenue declines, but relative market share could remain the same. Total market capitalization may decline, but relative market capitalization could remain the same if the markets deem your responses to the disruption appropriate. If management anticipates the disruption successfully, it could make adjustments that could result in limited negative impact on net profit and market share. Such a scenario for your Stakeholder Value Curve related to business financial performance could be depicted as in Figure 1-5.

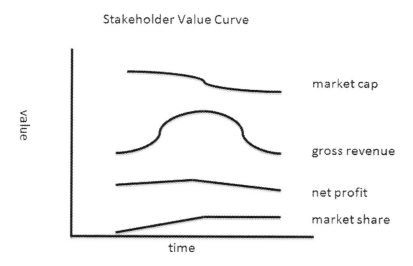

Figure 1-5: Your business stakeholder value curve incorporates several financial factors.

In this example, you could have a decline in your gross revenue and the markets could go down in general terms. But if you are successful in responding to a disruption such as a general market collapse, you can stabilize your net profit and relative market share, even though your total value declines with the stock market and gross revenues could decline with consumer spending.

Stakeholder value in the public sector can be more qualitative. For example, value to citizens is determined by their perception of their well being and could be described in the following terms:

- Quality of the environment
- Accessibility to services
- Safety from crime
- Quality of life
- Security from terrorism threats

The public sector can also have quantitative measurements such as:

- Budget deficits (surplus)
- Debt as a percentage of gross domestic product
- Trade deficits

In the social sector your value curve could be measured by the following factors that determine the quality of life for society:

- Percentage of population in poverty
- Percentage of population without health insurance
- Percentage of population un (under) employed
- Percentage of the population homeless
- Percentage of population dropping out of high school
- Percentage of students failing standardized tests

Your personal well-being could be measured in more intrinsic terms such as health, happiness or freedom from oppression. Being free from major disease or afflictions, or having stable, exciting, or meaningful personal relationships could contribute to happiness. The freedom from stress about layoffs or pressures at work contributes to your well being. Many people wake up every morning with the threat that someone is forcing them out of their homes, with the threat of arrest and persecution, or with the threat of violence on the way to school or to the community water well.

Over time these measures of value change as a result of disruptions. The attacks of 9/11 have been a major disruption resulting in wars on multiple fronts and a dramatic increase in security measures. These disruptions, which came on the heels of the dot-com market failure, have also contributed trillions of dollars to our budget deficits at the federal and state levels.

So, if America experienced a convergence of disrupters such as the dot-com market failure and the impact of terrorism and war, why did it still take eight years for the markets to collapse? The answer is that a "new gold rush" began in the form of real estate. Unfortunately, the basis for this gold rush was not finding value in the form of a precious metal discovery or new territory "reclaimed" from the indigenous population. Instead, value was created from market manipulation and fraudulent practices that were enabled by the repeal of the Glass Steagall Act in 1998.

The bill that opened the regulatory floodgates was called the Leach-Graham Congressional Bill. It was passed at the close of the 43rd Congress while legislators had airplane tickets in one hand and glad-handing good-byes in the other. It was officially called The Financial Services Modernization Act of 1999 (Public Law 106-102). Who in their right mind could argue against "modernization"? It was a quiet disrupter that opened the window of opportunity for financial institutions to create financial instruments such as credit default swaps that would have previously been off limits to most banks and savings and loans. The surge in the economy resulted from the over valued asset portfolios that were repackaged from marginal loans. Retirement funds and 401(k) accounts realized returns of historical proportions. But then the rate of value acceleration in the stock market fell off the shelf. Lessons learned from the savings and loan crisis of over reliance on under secured credit were evidently short-lived.

As an investor, business manager or citizen, this string of events has affected your value curve. There were many warning signs of these disruptions. In his book, *Fortune Favors the Bold*[27], Nobel Prize-winning economist Lester Thurow predicted a major "tipping point." He said that a blue ribbon panel of economic experts from the left and the right of the political spectrum agreed that there was going to be a major "adjustment." The only disagreement was about the severity: Republican economists predicted a rough landing, while Democratic economists predicted a crash-and-burn scenario. Thurow expected that there would have to be a 25 percent cut in GDP to make up for our past consumer appetites that have created massive trade deficits. That is like asking every person and corporation in the country to take a 25 percent cut in pay or profits. What politician has the guts to tell the American public to suck it up and tighten your belts three notches, with no relief in sight?

What is a Value Tipping Point?

In complexity theory there are many forces at work at any given time that impact your Stakeholder Value Curve. They are constantly interacting in a complex and adaptive environment. The changes in your stakeholder value curve are the result of trends that are observations of change over a period of time. When the degree of positive or negative change in your value curve changes direction, this is a tipping point. In math it is known as the inflection point, when the upward or downward slope of the curve is zero, or when the rate of acceleration turns zero. In terms of your value curve, this is a tipping point.

The first tipping point on a curve is when a value starts to increase significantly. In a business product life cycle this is often associated with the early adoption of a new technology or an invention. The early adopters are actively involved in predicting the future from recent and relevant trends. Recognizing the tipping point at stage 1 of a trend enables you to predict and project coming opportunities. The tipping point is often disguised as a challenge in its infant stage. The difference between a visionary and a dreamer is that the visionary recognizes the opportunity before everyone else and executes a plan. The greater the slope of the curve, the greater the acceleration of change will be, and therefore the greater potential for disruption to your industry or opportunity for your organization.

How long the "window of opportunity" exists varies, but it is typically shrinking faster in this hypercompetitive global economy. The availability of knowledge, talent and factors of production has become globally available. Digital accessibility makes diffusion of information instantaneous. The volatility of market changes and competitive forces make understanding and anticipating your tipping point more and more valuable for discovering windows of opportunity that open and close quickly.

Anticipating the Next Tipping Point

If you are waiting for an invitation to take advantage of a pending disruption, you will be the victim of the disruption and miss the window of opportunity. Imagine trying to escape through an automatic car window that is closing. I have seen it happen over and over in business, and it is not a pretty picture.

As shown in Figure 1-6, the first tipping point (TP 1) is when the increase in value first starts to accelerate. This is the beginning of the opportunity phase, when first mover advantages take hold and organizations enjoy little or no competition. Tipping Point 2 (TP 2) is when the rate of acceleration starts to decline but there is still growth. This occurs when there are some competitive forces in play and there is some erosion in market share, but limited impact on value, as defined by profit or market value.

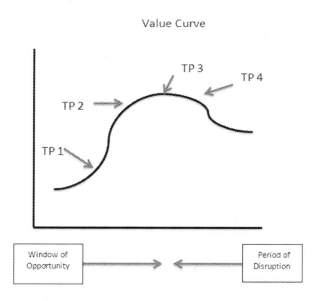

Figure 1-6: Tipping points offer a window of opportunity.

Tipping point 3 (TP 3) occurs when competition has had significant success and your value in terms of profit or market value starts to decline along with market share. At this point, your window of opportunity is closing. TP 3 is the first indication that your value proposition could be in jeopardy of falling into the competitive chasm.

At this point, rationalization is the norm. Stagnant revenue projections are explained away as a temporary shift in the financial markets. Or, it could be the failure of government to enact favorable legislation that your lobbyist promised was eminent. Concern for competitors' new product developments are minimized rather than anticipated as credible shifts in consumer preferences that demand different features, utility or functionality.

The question is this: did you take proactive measures to begin looking for new opportunities or did the disruption sneak up on you? The other question is: where are you on your value curve? Are you on the upside as a disrupter, taking advantage of the window of opportunity, or are you a laggard who let the downside of the curve surprise you? Of course, the panic phase starts in at TP 4, when the rate of decline starts to accelerate. All of your hopes and dreams start to spiral out of control. Bad decisions start to compound previously questionable decisions.

Some would argue that innovation should start at TP 3. At this stage, you have maximized the value from your current offering or product. I argue that you should always be in a state of renewal, but at a minimum innovation should occur between TP 2 and TP 3. You may not have a lot of time between TP2 and TP 3. By the time you get to TP 3, you are focused on retrenchment strategies such as cutting costs rather than growth opportunities. Innovation activities take a back seat as panic sets in and the stampede to the door intensifies as your best talent jumps ship. Fortunes can be made or lost and careers can blossom or collapse during these critical periods. As a business owner or as a manager, you must decide: will you jump ship into the murky waters, or stay on board to right the ship?

If you find your organization between TP 2 and TP 3, you are already in catch up mode. Your competition has probably introduced disruptive products or business models. When you look at the continuum of change, there is an upside and a downside. On the upside of the curve, you are riding the wave. You are taking advantage of change to grow and prosper. Alternatively, on the downside of the curve, you are the victim of change. Your products are obsolete. Your customers are fleeing to your competitors for better technology, value, or functionality. Profit margins are slipping, layoffs are looming, and bankruptcy is a growing threat.

On the macro level, the companies in your city or region are closing, your constituents are losing jobs, homes are in foreclosure, your tax base is declining, and schools are deteriorating from lack of capital. In other words, quality of life is spiraling down.

Usually, major shifts in industry value curves are caused by significant changes in environmental variables such as a technology breakthrough. It could be a scientific discovery or improvement that leads to new platforms and dominant technology standards. But, as we discuss in the next chapter, these disruptions could also come in the form of new market applications for existing products, or as innovations in the dominant business model of the industry that do not involve R&D advancement.

Entrepreneurship: The Art of Continuous Disruption

For entrepreneurs, disruption is inevitable and your response should be continuous. By definition an entrepreneur is a person who recognizes opportunities or challenges, creates innovative ideas and transforms them into goods and services that create economic or social value. Besides starting a new venture, the concept of entrepreneurship has been broadly extended into innovative activities within an existing business as well as social and public entities.

If you are the incumbent entrepreneur who is enjoying a first-mover advantage from an invention, you can expect disruption to occur as your competitors realize the value of your innovation. Imitation is the sincerest form of flattery. Your competitors will be very sincere in replicating your business model if you are successful.

You also can expect that the competitive advantage you may be enjoying in the growth stage of your innovation life cycle will get shorter as the hyper-competitive global economy provides opportunities for new competitors that did not exist 10 years ago. Consequently, it is important to constantly innovate to avoid a competitive chasm that may result in a decline from which you may not be able to recover.

If you are an emerging entrepreneur you should constantly look for tipping points in your strategic environment. Introducing innovations that cause disruptive technology products or business models should be a continual process of an innovation renaissance that can be the motivation for starting a new enterprise.

Not all new ventures focus on a new product from new and emerging technology. The rewards for successfully creating a new venture based on a new product patent can be substantial. However, one of the main points of this book is to extend innovation beyond the R&D that takes place in major corporate labs or that is licensed from university-sponsored research. Most entrepreneurs do not have labs to invent new technologies. Even if they license and commercialize new technology, the costs and risks can be overwhelming.

A number of major product shifts have occurred over the last few years. To practice your new role as Innovation Strategist, use the "Call to Action" as an exercise to plot your personal and industry value curve to help get you thinking about the next tipping point.

Call to Action

Develop your Personal Value Curve

1. Identify one of your personal value curves.
2. Plot the changes that have occurred over the past ten years and how you expect the value to change over the next ten years.
3. Where are you are on this value curve?
4. When is your next significant tipping point(s)?
5. Will it be a window of opportunity or period of disruption?

As an industry leader, can you identify and plot the changes in value related to your industry or your organization?

Call to Action

Develop your Industry Value Curve

1. What are the major disruptions that have impacted your industry in the past ten years?
2. What are the drivers of these disruptions?
3. What are the trends associated with these drivers of change?
4. Plot the market shares of the top five companies in your industrial sector.
5. Identify the tipping points and their causes along their value curves.
6. What do you anticipate as the next disruptions in your industry?
7. When do you expect the major tipping points to occur?
8. What trends will contribute to the major tipping points you anticipate?

In Figure 1-7 I have identified some of the current technologies, disrupters and emerging new products, as well as what may be next. Can you anticipate what is next for the other products?

Old Technology/ Product	Disrupters	New Technology/ Product	What's Next?
Printed books	Internet Diffusion	E-readers, tablets	Customized visual readers
Plain old telephone, Pagers	Infrastructure Bandwith (4G/ WiFi)	Smartphones, VOIP	Embedded chips
Video Rental stores		Streaming and Vending	Interactive TV
Bank tellers	Microprocessor Capacity	ATMs and Online Banking	RFID chips
Fax		Scan and e-mail	?
Video games	Social Media adoption	Interactive video games	?

Figure 1-7: Can you anticipate what is next?

Now you know that you can anticipate a future filled with disruptions. The next question is this: will your competitors disrupt you or will you intentionally create disruption?

CHAPTER 2

INTENTIONALLY CREATE DISRUPTION:
KEY #2

*"You cannot discover new oceans unless you have the courage
to lose sight of the shore." Anonymous*

Creative Disruption: A Proactive Innovation Strategy

The key to winning the future is successfully creating value in every activity you undertake. However, the process of value creation requires a proactive innovation strategy. With our hyper-competitive global economy evolving rapidly, this process of value creation must be continually renewed, refined, and reinvented. Business leaders and entrepreneurs must "venture away from the shore" to recognize and anticipate disruptions as opportunities for wealth creation, but most don't understand how to do this consistently.

Innovation research has focused more on the strategy of creating new technology breakthroughs, rather than developing business models to facilitate and formalize the innovation process for new and existing firms. Moreover, innovation strategy and opportunity identification have not been explored as a continuous process. Consequently the competitive advantages that come after initial venture developments quickly evaporate as disruptions shift economic fortunes. Without a strategy for renewal, successful entrepreneurs and leaders are continually at risk of losing their competitive advantage.

My research on this topic reveals a dramatic void when it comes to defining, formulating, or implementing an innovation strategy other than technological innovation. In this chapter, I suggest a new paradigm to fill this void—**Creative Disruption**—using an organic metaphor for developing a proactive and holistic innovation strategy for bridging the competitive chasms created by disruptions. Creative disruption serves as a unique resolution to the accelerating need for an innovation strategy that can be applied beyond R&D and product development. This new innovation strategy can apply to a wide range of strategic transformation activities, including technology development, strategic planning, business model renewal, and business process improvement.

The Disruption Continuum

As presented in the previous chapter, disruption can occur at many levels in the environment. The disruption continuum in Figure 2-1 illustrates the relative levels of magnitude of the disruptive impact on technology, industries, and organizations. At the radical end of the continuum is creative destruction caused by breakthrough technology. Creative disruption can result from moderate changes in the standard industry business model. On the incremental end strategic transformation occurs at the organizational level. At each stage of this continuum, a competitive chasm could emerge that can be an opportunity or challenge for your organization.

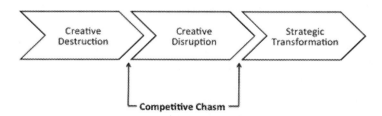

Figure 2-1: The disruption continuum illustrates disruptive impact on technology, industries, and organizations.

Creative destruction, an aging perspective championed by economist Joseph Schumpeter, has been credited as the foundation of entrepreneurship.

Schumpeter maintained that organizations and industries are destroyed when breakthrough technological disruption occurs. Entrepreneurs induce innovation to create new products, introduce new methods of production, open new markets, obtain new sources of raw materials, or create new business models. Entrepreneurs create value with radical innovation that causes technology discontinuity in the innovation life cycle. Schumpeter's theory concludes that this eventually leads to the creative destruction of industries.

This, however, is a very macro view. Not every technological innovation leads to the destruction of an industry. Sometimes periods of technological discontinuity—the displacement of one technology by another—occur instead. Technological discontinuity happens when new technology or breakthrough innovations advance, by an order of magnitude, the technological state of the art that characterizes an industry. Radical technology both enhances and destroys existing knowledge, just as innovations may either enhance or destroy existing competences.

Unfortunately, most existing firms investigate new technologies only after their core properties have reached the tipping point, creating a competitive chasm. Even when incumbent firms are responsible for technological innovation, they persist with investments in the current technologies because of the inertia caused by sunk costs.

For example, in the camera industry there was the innovation of the Polaroid Instant Camera. Their first mover advantage made their name synonymous with the instant print technology. But they could not adjust to the creative destruction caused by the digital camera and went bankrupt in 2005.

Then there was Eastman Kodak, whose researchers invented the digital camera, but failed to capitalize on first mover advantages. In fact, their CEO, Antonio Perez called it a "crappy" business because of narrow margins. They have had to sell or license their digital imaging patent portfolio after years of attempts at a turnaround from a shrinking, film-based company to a growing digital one. Kodak in 2010 also had a one-time windfall of $210 million from patent licensing.

Now Kodak is looking to change their business model similarly to Apple with online photo sharing (Kodak Gallery) and a new technology called "Scan the World" that is designed to digitize old photos. As 2011 closes, however, Kodak has filed bankruptcy indicating their attempts to reinvent their business model have not been successful.

Bridging the Competitive Chasm

Does an industry have to become extinct before we notice the potential business opportunities created by technological disruptions and subsequent market discontinuities? That is comparable to waiting for the big tsunami and ignoring all the tremors that portend pending disaster. Quite often, a series of competitive chasms occur, eventually leading to breakthrough disruptions.

Because of their sunk costs, incumbent firms have little economic incentive to switch when new technology is first introduced. Additionally, they are concerned about cannibalizing their existing markets and products. Sometimes managers are so enamored with their products, or face internal organizational obstacles to changing core technology, that they ignore or do not recognize the emerging threat. They often respond with incremental product improvement.

Ideally, entrepreneurial firms try to proactively introduce innovation without waiting for core technologies to reach a tipping point. A model for formalizing and expediting the innovation process is needed to facilitate creative entrepreneurial opportunities. Innovation needs to be accelerated to keep up with the rapidly growing competitive challenges in the global economy. Improving this process is important to entrepreneurs and managers because it provides an opportunity to anticipate and bridge competitive chasms, particularly in the technological environment, in order to create opportunities for wealth and sustainable competitive advantage.

One of the keys to sustainable innovation is to intentionally create disruption in order to bridge the competitive chasm caused by these technological disruptions. Creative disruption is a proactive approach to innovation which looks for opportunities as a matter of continuous and institutionalized effort, rather than randomly and passively reacting to market shifts. It is a systematic approach to exploring and exploiting opportunities for growth, development, and productivity in your internal and external value creating activities, relationships, and interactions. Creative disruption can result in changes in the prevailing business model for an industry as a result of the introduction of less radical technology or innovation.

Exploiting or initiating creative disruptions at all levels of your environment will accelerate the pace of the innovation life cycle in your favor. Adopting a creative disruption mentality allows you to thrive on discontinuities of technology and markets. It helps you anticipate the next big thing and sustain your competitive advantage. This perspective will ensure you are victor rather than the victim of competitive chasms.

The Disruptive Innovation Life Cycle

A disruptive innovation is one that creates technological discontinuity in the market or industry but does not require a major change in technology standards or destroy an industry as in the creative destruction paradigm.

Consistent with our ecosystem metaphor, product ecology theory uses S-curves to depict the product life cycle. As seasons change, vegetation sprouts, grows, ripens, and decays if not harvested. In business ecosystems, an industry or firm evolves through a succession of technology or innovation life cycles, with each cycle beginning with technological disruption. These technological disruptions, whether radical or incremental, cause economic instability by threatening established businesses and providing opportunities for new businesses. If the changes are radical, they can bring about creative destruction from an industry perspective, as Schumpeter theorized. From a firm level, radical disruptions can be competency destroying, in the sense that they make existing knowledge and intellectual property advantages obsolete.

In the S-curve of the Innovation Life Cycle (see Figure 2-2), the value of an innovation is plotted over time. The first area under the curve as you move along the x-axis is often indicative of a market niche attributable to first mover advantages. Value creation evolves into a competitive advantage up to the next tipping point. At this part of the curve, the rate of value increase reaches zero and then begins to decline. If the organization initiates an incremental innovation, represented by the small dotted curve, the life cycle of the innovation is extended. The gap in time represents a competitive chasm during which there is a loss of total value.

In Figure 2-2 we see the innovation life cycles when an enterprise attempts to increase its value by taking a proactive approach to creative disruption. In the short S-curve, the organization initiates an incremental innovation. In the longer and upward sloping S-curve, the value is a radical or disruptive innovation. The significant crossover point, called a "paradigm shift," which occurs when something with technological potential becomes a market phenomenon.

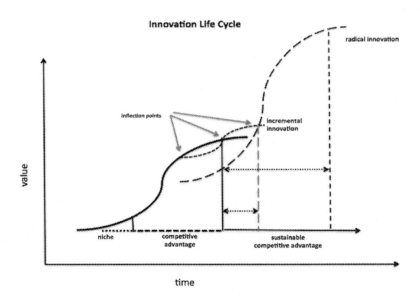

Figure 2-2: The Innovation Life Cycle illustrates how innovation can be extended.

On the other hand, radical innovation can represent a moment of creative disruption at which point the rate of increase in value increases exponentially. If the innovation results in resources that are inimitable as confirmed by intellectual property rights, it could represent a sustainable competitive advantage. Using this concept of an innovation life cycle also allows for a quantitative approach to maximizing the return on innovation investment as well.

Many firms experience periods of munificence associated with value creating innovations. As the rate of industry growth declines, environmental uncertainty regarding the continued value of the innovation intensifies. This uncertainty may be caused by the introduction of new patents prior to market introduction. In addition, countervailing forces such as regulatory restraints or social paradigm shifts may eventually lead to the onset of discontinuities. If there are periods during which the entrepreneur is not innovating, they are subject to the environmental uncertainties that may eventually lead to technological discontinuities. Anticipating and bridging these competitive chasms with new product or process innovation creates new periods of environmental growth and opportunities for wealth creation.

One key is not only whether the core technical expertise of an industry is disrupted by an innovation, but also whether links in the value chain are overturned or reinforced by the new technology. The inability to adapt to a new technical standard kills more firms than the inability to withstand a recession. Additionally, technological disruptions affect market shares by altering the established barriers to entry and upward mobility in an industry. The time for detecting the need to change is limited by the market growth of the new product and the speed of its diffusion between users.

As we progress into the new millennium, we should expect the frequency of technological discontinuities to increase, and as such, proactive companies will have the advantage over reactionary firms. Consequently, entrepreneurs must find breakthrough technologies to sustain their competitive advantage. However, a radical innovation is a true breakthrough technology only if people accept it and use it to change the way they work and live. For example, AT&T researchers invented the voice compression technology that enabled Internet telephone calls, but the company was slow to penetrate the voice over Internet protocol (VOIP) market. Companies such as Skype and Vonage have capitalized on this technology with their business models.

Disruption in the American Automobile Industry

An example of a disruptive innovation life cycle is the market myopia of the American automotive industry. American carmakers enjoyed a substantial competitive advantage for decades, until Japanese automakers started improving their value through offering better quality vehicles in the late 1980s and early 1990s. Many attribute the Japanese automakers' turnaround to the incremental innovation of total quality management and statistical process control methods introduced by Edward Deming.

Figure 2-2 could also represent the disruptive life cycle of the automobile industry. The first tipping point in the curve represents the point at which the rate of growth in market share for American automakers started to decline. Because they were still profitable, American automakers continued to produce gas guzzling trucks and SUVs, while Japanese auto makers started to introduce hybrids, represented by the long upward curve of radical innovation. Because there was not a strong market, American automakers did not introduce alternative energy cars. Instead, firms like Chrysler proudly promoted bigger, less-fuel-efficient cars like the Hemi 5.7 liter engine, popularized by the ad slogan, "You got a Hemi under there?" Another incremental innovation was adding more cup holders in their mini vans. Represented by the short curve, these incremental innovations represent the market myopia of the American automobile makers.

Of course this could one day be the story of other industries such as the oil industry. As of 2011 Exxon-Mobil, Chevron, and ConocoPhillips represent the second, third, and fourth largest American corporations. If there is a major disruption in the energy industry, with breakthrough technology this could result a major shift in global wealth. It could also mean that the Arab Spring could topple wealthy monarchies in countries such as Saudi Arabia, Kuwait, and the Arab Emirates. Major oil exporters such as Iran may face economic realities that destabilize their economies and the political dynamics of the Middle East.

When the gas crisis hit around the time of Hurricane Katrina, the market for hybrids started to accelerate as the market for inefficient gas-guzzlers declined. By the time the financial crisis of 2008 hit, American automakers were in a free fall toward bankruptcy. Rising fuel prices made it even more difficult for GM to recover. General Motors survived only because of the federal bailout and bankruptcy that allowed them to restructure the benefit packages of their retired workers and other legacy costs.

I remember watching Rick Wagoner, GM's CEO at the time, when he was interviewed by *60 Minutes* at the 2006 Auto Show. In this segment he dismissed the threat of Indian and Chinese market entries based on their lack of environmental features such as the catalytic converter that is required in the U.S. He must have thought it would it take too long for Chinese engineers to retrofit their cars as necessary. He also pinned their market hopes on one vehicle—the Volt. I could not help but criticize his myopic view, which did not take into account the global trends of rising fuel costs and growing environmental concerns. Is this the caliber of innovation management leading what used to be the second largest corporation in the world? Of course Wagoner's tenure was short-lived after that.

As 2012 begins we find out that General Motors regained its title as the world's top-selling automaker after its 2009 taxpayer-funded bankruptcy restructuring allowed it to cut its spiraling legacy costs. It has also helped that Toyota's sales decline because of production cuts following a massive recall, an earthquake, a tsunami, a nuclear crisis in Japan, and deadly floods in Thailand. But is GM in a position to withstand normal competitive pressure? Already in 2012 they have started to curtail the production of the Volt because of weak demand and product failures.

Diminishing Returns on Innovation Investment

Businesses are grappling with the question of how much to invest in innovation. To answer this question, we must consider which level of innovation provides the best return. Of course, the "home run" of the breakthrough technological innovation can create the largest value, but, based on the probability of success and the cost of the investment, this may not lead to the greatest return. In fact, a recent study by Booze Allen and Hamilton (BAH) challenged the assumption that the return on investment of technological innovation is better than other types of innovation investment. BAH's analysis of global personal care and consumer healthcare companies showed no clear correlation between R&D spending as a percentage of sales and growth in revenues or profitability. This focus is too narrow and fails to take into account incremental innovation on an existing product or technology that could lead to a new application creating a new market or business model.

The BAH study also found that incremental innovation investments are subject to diminishing returns. Resources are wasted on increasingly marginal projects. The Oreo cookie is an example of how incremental product innovations based on minimal feature changes produce marginal returns. Although we celebrate the 100th birthday of the Oreo in 2012, for the majority of customers it still gets down to pulling the cookie apart first. Attempts to improve on the basic product can produce returns that are barely noticeable as graphically illustrated in figure 2-3:

Marginal Returns on Innovation
The Oreo Effect

Oreo

Oreo mint

Oreo white fudge

Oreo Easter

Oreo Halloween

Oreo piecrust

Oreo ice cream cones

Oreo double stuff

Oreo banana split

Oreo Shrek

Oreo Grinch

Oreo cakester

Figure 2-3: Incremental innovation investments can have decreasing marginal returns.

The solution to innovation anemia is not to boost incremental spending, but to raise the *effectiveness* of innovation investment. So how do we determine the effectiveness of innovation investment to achieve both breakthrough innovations and value-added incremental innovation? One approach is to measure the optimal values associated with innovation calculus.

The Calculus of Innovation

As you consider the life cycle of innovation and how to maximize your ROI, one important question should come to mind: when is the optimum point when an organization should make a serious effort in innovation, whether it is technology, business model or a business process? The answer to this question can be quantified using the Innovation Life Cycle (Fig 2-2). By plotting the value of your product in terms of revenue or marginal profit, the tipping point that was mentioned earlier predicts when the increase in value will start to decline. At this point, you must initiate a new value curve.

By applying calculus to projected stakeholder value curves, you can determine whether a firm should invest in incremental improvements to extend a product life, or make major investments in a radical technology. If your projections are reliable, you can calculate the area under the curve and compare the value of the innovation alternatives using the following definite integral formula:

$$\int_a^b f(x)dx$$

A comparison of value curve areas can help determine the optimal investment strategy as well as timing of the investment. Of course, you must consider the time value of money by using formulas such as discounted cash flow and the internal rate of return to calculate the return on investment associated with the value curve.

As we reach new limits in technological innovation, it becomes increasingly costly to make progress. At the same time, the possibility of new approaches often emerges. Proactive entrepreneurs, particularly incumbent firms, must continually scan their environment to understand the innovation cycle represented by the S-curve and anticipate competitive chasms.

The Hierarchy of Innovation

Most definitional typologies describe innovation in terms of radical or incremental, and usually from the perspective of technology. Another way of looking at innovation can be in terms of a hierarchy. Tremendous value creation opportunities can be realized by viewing innovation beyond R&D. Specifically value can be achieve by innovation efforts at the strategic, business model, and business process levels, as shown in Figure 2-3

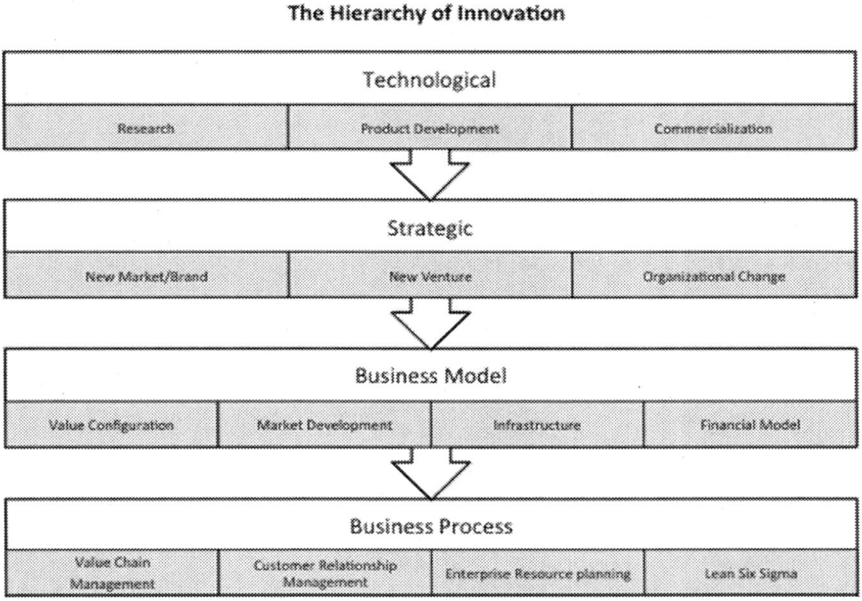

The Hierarchy of Innovation

Technological		
Research	Product Development	Commercialization

Strategic		
New Market/Brand	New Venture	Organizational Change

Business Model			
Value Configuration	Market Development	Infrastructure	Financial Model

Business Process			
Value Chain Management	Customer Relationship Management	Enterprise Resource planning	Lean Six Sigma

Figure 2-4: Innovation can be viewed in terms of a strategic hierarchy.

Technological innovation can be radical, disruptive, incremental or breakthrough depending on the degree of impact on the technical standards in the industry. Innovations based on breakthrough technology can build on the firm's existing competencies or make them obsolete. It is mostly conducted in research and development laboratories for the purpose of technology commercialization.

A central premise of this book is that innovation can be applied to other areas of your efforts to transform your organization. Strategic Innovation can change an organization's marketing and branding strategy, create new venture spin-offs, and major organization change projects. Business Model innovation focuses on value configuration, market development, infrastructure, and financial models. Business Process innovation involves value chain management, customer relationship management, enterprise resource planning, and lean six-sigma activities. We first analyze technological disruption using an example from the smartphone industry.

The Smartphone Industry: A Tipping Point of Technological Disruption?

A good example of an industry that could be at a tipping point of technological disruption is the smartphone industry. The source of this disruption is the multi-touch technology that flips and spins at the touch of a finger. Apple filed patents for this technology at the end of 2007 when it first introduced the iPhone. In the middle of 2011 Apple was awarded the patent on the multi-touch on mobile devices. As late as December 2011 a court ruled that HTC was in violation of this patent.

What does this mean for the many smartphone and tablet competitors? Apple could sue to ban all imports of similar devices. Or competitors will be forced to pay Apple a royalty fee for every device they sell. Companies like Samsung and HTC are now the disrupted that could be on the brink of a competitive chasm. This technology is also built into Apple's track pads and mice. It would be hard to consider buying a smartphone or tablet without it. So what is the next move for the smartphone competitors?

Apple has also acquired C3 Technologies to add realistic looking 3D maps to their iPhone. Currently Apple uses Google Maps, a dependency that the late Steve Jobs could not have been pleased with given his penchant for end-to-end control of his technology. Experts predict that this declassified missile guidance technology, which renders detail of buildings, trees and even smaller objects, will allow Apple to develop a new technology standard on its next generation of iPhone. Of course, the genius of Jobs lives on with the introduction of Siri, an artificial intelligence application introduced on the newly released iPhone 4S.

Beyond Technological Innovation

Obviously high risk and high reward possibilities come with technological innovation. One of the central themes of this book is that a holistic approach to creating an innovation system should apply to more than just R&D or new product development. Apple had already created a market for its iPod using a complementary music standard, MP3 that it did not invent. But by using enhanced software algorithms for its iTunes store it was able to maximize its technological advances.

For too long, the common misconception has been that innovation is the sole province of scientist and engineers. Moving innovation beyond R&D requires a new model for strategic transformation activities; a model based on opportunity recognition and exploitation activities.

Strategic innovation focuses on products or services that may be disruptive or sustaining, but do not necessarily involve new technology. It could involve a new market or a new market application. Strategic innovations, on the other hand, can also lead to the development of a new brand. New ideas that generate new ventures can result in spin-offs of a new firm if not perceived as part of the firm's original core competence.

The Strategic Transformation Model

So how do you move beyond R&D to create sustainable value at the strategic and business model level? You should take a holistic approach to change, as embodied in The Strategic Transformation Model. This kind of essential change can be affected at the macro or micro level of the environment, where it can be both discontinuous and comprehensive.

At the macro level creative disruption can take the form of strategic foresight, product development, and strategic planning. Visionary leaders who embrace and advance new ideas within their environments and organizations will drive this powerful approach.

This comprehensive approach to strategic innovation can revolutionize the way we pursue growth and value creation. To be successful, businesses and industries should position business model innovation at the critical intersection of opportunity recognition and opportunity exploitation, as seen in Figure 2-4.

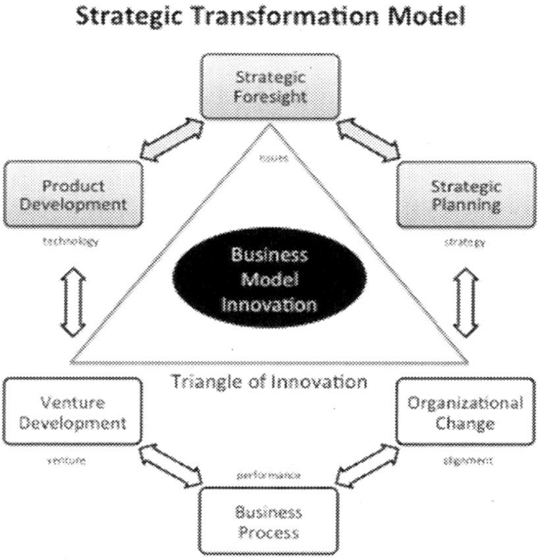

Figure 2-5: The Strategic Transformation Model provides a holistic approach to sustainable innovation.

Where to Target your Creative Disruption?

The Triangle of Innovation (see Figure 2-4) should be the target of your creative disruption activities. It encompasses the opportunity recognition activities in the top half of the Strategic Transformation Model. Innovation can also occur during opportunity exploitation, which is represented by the bottom half of the model. More radical change that can result in a sustainable competitive advantage occurs in the Triangle of Innovation.

Opportunity recognition is commonly defined as the perception of an organization's potential to create a profitable new venture or improve the strategic position of an existing business. Rather than a discrete and random event, opportunity recognition is more often an emergent process driven by organizational learning. Opportunity recognition skills allow managers and stakeholders to anticipate technological disruptions and discontinuities in existing markets.

Nature dictates that humans will, unless stimulated otherwise, address issues that are temporally current and within their control. It usually takes external stimulus to change one's everyday task agenda to a futurist perspective that reflects strategic planning and visioning activities. The process of strategic planning has been well documented and explored in textbooks, research, and practice.

Strategic visioning has long been the "fuzzy front end" of discovery and is therefore challenging to formulate and implement. For example, how many people could foresee the social networking epidemic sweeping the globe? MySpace was first but Facebook succeeded. Simon was first, but iPhone set the standard for smartphones. The white space in front of a new market is always very fuzzy. Sometimes the technology exists but the value of an opportunity comes in the form of recognizing applications and markets.

These applications of opportunity discovery are important to an organization's attempt to grow and add value for its stakeholders. They exemplify how stakeholders and leaders in a variety of industries and organizations can be proactive and search out opportunities for transformation, rather than wait for the proverbial knock on the door that will probably never come.

Strategic Foresight

Opportunity recognition at the macro level starts with strategic foresight initiatives by think tanks and planning agencies. These groups typically address long-term planning at the macro level for public policy and regional economic development, anticipating social and regulatory issues and developing plans associated with these issues.

The Institute for Innovation has been involved in the strategic foresight efforts of the Brazilian government. The Brazilians enacted a federal statute called the Law of Innovation 2005 to accelerate innovation throughout the country. We have worked on two strategic foresight projects with the Center for Strategic Studies (CGEE), which is responsible for developing industry level plans for the Ministry of Science and Technology.

CGEE assembles scientist, economists, and regulators from around the country to identify global, national, and industrial trends that point to future disruptions and opportunities. The Institute for Innovation facilitates brainstorming session to help CGEE stakeholders discover ideas, and develop scenarios and technological road maps for their clients. The results for two previous engagements have been published in prospective reports for the advanced materials and photovoltaic sectors of the Brazilian economy.

At the regional international level, the European Commission engages stakeholders from European Union (EU) countries in strategic foresight activities based on future oriented technology analyses, forecasting studies and technology assessment. Strategic foresight allows the commission to understand future opportunities and challenges in the global environment. The foresight conferences that the EU sponsors also provide a framework for collaboration to address common issues that have future implications. This process enables policy makers to make better decisions at the macro level for EU constituents.

There is considerable research that indicates using strategic foresight at the corporate level to effectively anticipate technical and market disruption is a crucial competence in today's hyper-competitive environment, but many companies are ignoring this truth. According to a study by the European Commission on Foresight, companies have built strong capabilities for collecting information, but lack the ability to interpret information, disseminate gained insights and trigger management reactions. [28] In this study, only 23 percent of the participants state that strategic foresight insights are rapidly diffused, which implies that future insights might not reach the appropriate decision makers. The study further indicates that 46 percent of companies do not have adequate method portfolios, limiting their ability to interpret information. Only 28 percent of companies regularly challenge basic assumptions, and are therefore alert to disruptive changes in their environment.

In a recent Bain survey, 70 percent of the companies said their business transformation initiatives did not deliver the expected results.[29] This dismal success rate has remained unchanged from similar surveys they conducted in the 1980s and 1990s. One reason for these poor results could be the lack of a systematic approach to the strategic transformation process. What we need is a way to incorporate a holistic approach to innovation to improve value creation. Top performing companies invest significantly more resources in gathering data from restricted sources. They utilize qualitative methods and purposely employ methodology. Top performing companies also tend to engage in more foresight activities that include all levels of the organization to raise the level of alertness as well as their scanning reach and scope. These findings suggest the need to engage hierarchical diversity in the transformation processes. This means that more than top management should be involved in the planning process.

Strategic foresight activities can be a tremendous boost to signaling key opportunities for new product development and strategic planning at the organizational level. Well planned visioning projects can produce scenario that articulate desired futures. Other visioning outputs can include strategic and technology roadmaps that articulate gaps in technology development, human capital, infrastructure, and financial resources. These roadmaps can help organizations focus their new product development and strategic planning efforts.

New Product Development

New product development (NPD) is the business area most typically associated with technological innovation. At the industry level, ideas could be generated by strategic foresight activities within think tanks, development agencies, innovation clusters, and cooperative alliances. At the organizational level it involves research and development and technology commercialization in the form of disruptive, radical, and breakthrough technology generated from an organization's corporate foresight or strategic planning activities.

NPD could also mean incremental or process innovation that makes the product lighter or faster, or gives it more throughput or bandwidth. It could also incorporate technology commercialization at the industry level of the environment. These innovation activities can obviously impact your overall business model innovation strategy.

Research organization such as universities that transfer technology typically have a portfolio of great ideas that have come out of their labs, sometimes funded by The National Science Foundation, The National Institutes of Health, or private research and development. However, much of this technology is sitting on a shelf because entrepreneurs do not understand the technology nor recognize the opportunity for commercialization. Holistic innovation will help organizations bring scientists and entrepreneurs together and brainstorm using this treasure trove of great ideas. (Case studies for technology commercialization are provided in Chapter 9).

The Fuzzy Front End of Innovation

The "fuzzy front end" of innovation is where the organization formulates a concept of the product to be developed and decides whether to invest resources in the further development of an idea. The fuzzy front end is the phase between the first consideration of an opportunity and when it is determined to be ready for the structured development process. It includes all activities from the search for new opportunities, through the formation of a germ of an idea, to the development of a precise concept.

The fuzzy front end concludes when an organization approves and begins formal development of the concept. Although the fuzzy front end may not be an expensive part of product development, it can consume 50 percent of development time. It is also where major resource commitments are and the product's nature is defined.

This portion of the innovation cycle is the uncertain period of new product development processes. Of course, any new product or innovation needs a business to evolve in order to go to market and create value. Organizations need to work through this fuzzy front end to come up with ideas that can be vetted using the business model framework.

According to research by business innovation scholar and lecturer Peter Koen, there are several front-end elements (not necessarily in a particular order): [30]

- Opportunity Identification: Identifying breakthrough or incremental strategies and technologies
- Opportunity Analysis: Identifying opportunities for business and technology implications by aligning ideas to target customer groups, and conducting market studies and technical trials and research
- Idea Genesis: Maturing the opportunity into a tangible idea
- Idea Selection: Choosing whether to pursue an idea by analyzing its potential business value.

The focus of innovation is the commercialization of new products ideas. This book is designed to provide a reliable and systematic approach that accelerates the process, beginning with opportunity identification. This approach incorporates research on trends and driving forces that indicate future possibilities that can eventually lead to new idea creation and commercialization. The commercialization phase of NPD involves identifying new market applications from new technology and creating road maps for implementation. From the perspective of NPD, business model innovation is one of the core elements of determining a successful market disruption.

Strategic Planning

Innovation is a critical element of corporate strategic planning, which has been around for quite some time. The standard strategic planning paradigm includes environmental analysis, strategy formulation, strategy implementation, and evaluation.

The typical strategic formulation process involves developing a mission, vision, goals, and objectives, as shown in Figure 2-5. These high-level planning concepts also include key success factors, action plans and evaluation tools. Too often, this process happens at the "40,000 foot level" and can be difficult to translate into functional-level activities.

Figure 2-6: The typical strategic planning process

As is the case for new product development, strategic planning at the organizational level can be inspired by national, regional, or industrial strategic foresight efforts. In our Strategic Transformation Model (see Figure 2-4), these planning outputs can generate new value propositions for a different business model.

Results from a strategic plan can include the following:

- Mergers and acquisitions
- Joint ventures
- International expansion
- New product application
- New brand development
- New market development
- New pricing strategy
- New distribution channels
- Outsourcing strategy
- New advertising strategy
- Customer service strategy
- Capital acquisition strategy

All of these elements are important for success.

Opportunity Exploitation

The natural progression in The Strategic Transformation Model is that opportunity recognition leads to opportunity exploitation. This is an important phase of innovation implementation, whether you use an external or internal approach. Once opportunities are recognized from product development, the logical progression is to commercialize it. That can come in the form of a new venture spin off. Also, if an internal approach is warranted, an organization change or business process improvement project can be initiated.

A new venture plan could involve a new wholly owned subsidiary, a joint venture, or licensing arrangement. Mergers and acquisitions can be used to execute a new venture strategy for acquiring competitors or strategic complementaries and partners with new technology or business method patents. New partnerships and strategic alliances must be developed to enhance core capabilities. New target markets and customer relationships must be cultivated. Revenue sources must be developed and profit margins must be refined.

To exploit opportunity from your strategic plan, your internal innovation strategy requires organizational renewal. In the organization change and development process you acquire new equipment and systems. Employees must be trained on the new technology and processes. New evaluation, control and incentive systems must be put in place. New supplier and distributor relationships must be developed to accommodate value chain adjustments. New organization structures must be devised which sometimes requires a culture shift to make the organization more organic in accommodating change.

Opportunity exploitation can also take place at the very micro level of business process improvements. Business process innovations consist of small modifications or refinements to pre-existing processes or phenomenological states such as existing policies, procedures, product line, and services. These innovations also manifest as improvements in operations and cost control, as well as in the product or service performance necessary to keep pace with competitors. Incremental innovation is a common focus in organizations when their innovation life cycle reaches the maturity stage. Companies implement strategies to extend the life of the product with upgrades and new releases, if forecasts indicate some remaining profitability. This strategy may allow the product to continue through the decline stage without further investments.

Business process improvement often involves the innovation of the value network (Figure 2-6) and other critical systems. The value network is an intricate balance of internal and external stakeholder relationships. It starts with the value chain that describes the relationships between primary functions such inbound, process, outbound marketing, and customer service. The secondary activities are support functions such as information technology, procurement, engineering, administration, research and development, administration, finance, and human resources. The value network expands the value chain internal functions to include relationships with the external stakeholders such as stockholders, investors, auditors, customers, complementors, intermediaries, outsource contractors, suppliers, and laboratories. Complementors are businesses that directly sell a product or service that adds value to mutual customers of another company. For example, Microsoft's Windows OS, Intel's Pentium processor, and McAfee's anti-virus products are complementors to personal computer manufacturers.

If optimized, these relationships should function efficiently as in an ecosystem I described in earlier chapters. The efficiency of the actors and their relationship within the external environment need natural and engineered systems to optimize output and growth. With optimally designed structures that provide for permeable boundaries, these systems should facilitate the flow of information between all business functions and internal stakeholders. They should also optimize the many connections to outside stakeholders.

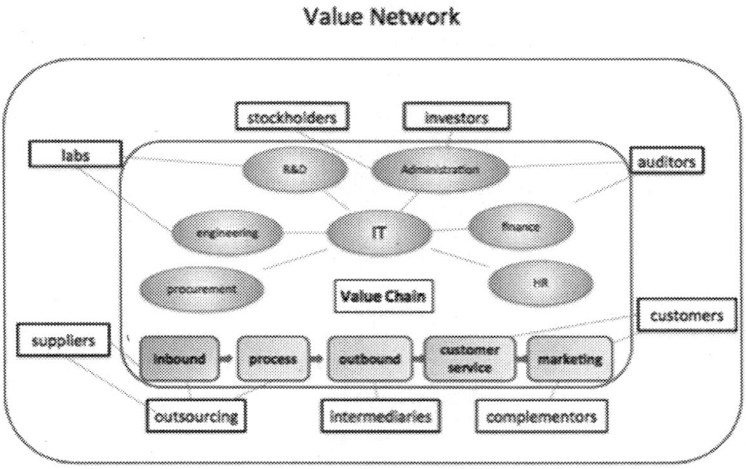

Value Network

Figure 2-7: The Value Network Analysis describes internal and external stakeholder business process relationships

At the heart of the value network are information technology (IT) systems such as the following:

- Enterprise Resource Planning (ERP): a computer system that integrates internal and external management information. It typically includes finance, accounting, manufacturing, sales and service, supply chain management, and project management.
- Customer Relationship Management: a strategy for managing the company's interactions with customers, clients, and prospects.
- Lean Six-Sigma: a strategy for improving the quality of process outputs by identifying and removing the causes of errors in any internal process or external relationship.

Most of these opportunity exploitation activities require a significant investment of time and resources. The key to successful innovation is to convert opportunities into value by creating a sustainable business model. This business model is the logical framework for a successful transition between opportunity recognition and opportunity exploitation.

CHAPTER 3

Inspire Creative Intelligence: Key #3

"If the bee disappears from the surface of the earth, man would have no more than four years to live. No more bees, no more pollination ... no more men!"—Albert Einstein

Creative Leaders: The Honeybees of Innovation

Although honeybees pollinate 70 percent of our food source, their importance in the global ecosystem goes beyond honey production. They represent the essence of value creation in nature. At one point some experts predicted that the sudden disappearance of 30 percent of the honeybee population in one year would lead to a major disruption in our food chain.

Make no mistake! Creative Leaders are the honeybees of our economic ecosystem. The "pollination" conducted by creative thought leaders produces an innovative culture of interdependent environments, energy and actors. The increase in R&D outsourcing and the decline in STEM graduates in the U.S. -- representing a decline in the investment and output of innovation -- are equivalent to the disappearing honeybees.

The third key to sustainable innovation is to inspire creative leadership. In this innovation ecosystem productive colonies of creative leaders are need to serve as the pollinators of creativity among their stakeholders. Instead we have gross generalizations based on the celebration of a few innovative celebrities. Steve Jobs of Apple was one such pollinator. Perceived as the epitome of creativity, innovation and vision, he personally reviewed every creative idea at Apple. Employees pitched ideas like gladiators to the emperor who had the power to give it a "thumbs up or down." And his passion for creativity in design and function helped bring Apple back from the abyss. But the passing of Steve Jobs not only reminds us of his genius, but the precariousness of relying on the creative talent of one person. Maybe the model of the lone creative genius as innovation leader, in the vein of Edison, Bell or Jobs is outdated. I believe innovative leadership must be a quality dispersed throughout an organization to empower and inspire all stakeholders—from top to bottom as well as inside out. We need more honeybees in a thriving colony.

This chapter focuses on the "soil and seeds" of an innovation ecosystem. An innovation culture requires a core of inspired innovation stakeholders with creative leadership skills. Understanding the basic components of creativity can help nourish innovative minds throughout your organization's ecosystem. That increases the absorption rate of knowledge into the innovation system, which, in turn, fosters the growth associated with knowledge creation. That increased rate of absorption of knowledge into the innovation ecosystem fosters growth and value creation.

This book provides specific guidance on how to empower innovation stakeholders to become Innovations Strategists by identifying innovation styles, helping develop their creative skills, and making sure they are well utilized within the organization. Also, some of the characteristics of innovative leaders will be described as well as how they manage an innovation culture.

Going Gaga for Creativity

From kindergarten on, most of us were conditioned not to make trouble, to get along and to conform. But creative minds typically belong to nonconformists with inspired and often unruly imaginations.

When *Fast Company* magazine did a feature on "The 100 Most Creative People in Business,"[31] pop artist Lady Gaga topped the list. At age 24 she has created a brand and a business conglomerate that converges Madison

Avenue with Wall Street. Her meteoric rise in popularity is a great example of turning creativity into innovation by identifying needs, exploiting opportunities and creating products as well as a brand.

Lady Gaga's signature flamboyant fashion statement resonates with a generation that craves shocking stimulus. She has responded to this generation's interest in social responsibility by creating a lipstick that has raised $2.2 million for AIDS awareness. She has mastered the social media with over 3.8 million followers on Twitter. Her dancing talents have gone viral using the You Tube media. She has even branded her fans as "little monsters." What can we learn from Lady Gaga? Being creative in a hyper-competitive environment means building a brand and a business model targeted toward modern trends and non-traditional media.

Hannah Jones of Nike was cited by *Fast Company* for a business model that relies on the convergence of strategic partnerships outside of the athletic footwear industry that focus on energy. For example, she has partnered Nike with NASA and venture capitalists to address water shortages. She has also partnered with Creative Commons to launch GreenXchange, a platform for sharing green intellectual property. Open Collaboration Lab is a partnership between Nike and PopTech for scientists and engineers involved in renewable energy innovation.

K.R. Sridhar used technology he designed for converting water into oxygen on Mars into Bloom Box. This is a refrigerator-size, emissions-free power station that uses natural gas or bio-fuels to generate as much electricity as a coal plant.

But creativity is just the starting point. Millions of creative people and hundreds of creative inventors did not make the list. For creativity to generate financial or social value, it must be turned into something tangible by recognizing an opportunity.

Creativity: The New Currency of Human Capital

Creativity is the process that generates invention, which can subsequently result in innovation. It also determines an entrepreneur's innovative response to external changes and opportunity. Within an organization, creativity is a function of the social processes, structure, and incentives that shape how individuals interact. When an organization proactively and systematically introduces the process of creativity, this results in the valuable currency of human and intellectual capital. This currency comes in the form of innovative stakeholders, innovative leadership and innovation systems.

The 21st Century will be dominated by organizations that create a sustainable competitive advantage by excelling in the development of human capital. This is in stark contrast to the importance of land and labor capital in previous economic systems. Competitive organizations are those that will master the art of knowledge creation as part of organizational learning processes. Creative leadership focuses on developing social and human capital by investing in the firm's internal knowledge development.

Employee creativity is a critical element of an organization's human capital. Research suggests employee creativity evolves into a collective intelligence system with appropriate collaboration by stakeholders. This system must be based on an iterative process that is cross-disciplinary and is highly influenced by the organization's social-cultural context.[32] An intentional approach to creativity must deconstruct and reconstruct the concept as proposed by my model called the "the Seven I's of Creative Intelligence."

The Seven I's of Creative Intelligence

One of the mysterious, yet essential elements of innovation is the human mind and the ability of our creative intelligence to yield innovation. All humans have the innate ability to think and form images and thoughts, which leads to creating original ideas. An individual's creative ability is determined by intellectual abilities, knowledge, and styles of thinking, personality, motivation, and environment.

Creative Intelligence is an innovative thinking process that involves the purposeful mental manipulation of information to form concepts, engage in problem solving, reason, and make decisions. Creative intelligence leads to creativity, which is the manifestation of ideas into a productive form. Creativity is the originating point of innovation and is the basic component of the human capital in an organization that inspires the value creation process.

The Seven I's of Creative Intelligence are the building blocks of creativity. They manifest as abstract and concrete elements of the human mind (See Figure 3-1).

1. **Inspiration** is the stimulation of the human mind with knowledge and other environmental stimulus to generate creative thought and inspire the imagination to actualize new ideas.
2. **Imagination** is the ability to visualize and form images and ideas in the mind.
3. **Insight** is the ability to arrive at an understanding of the images and ideas in the human mind based on identification of relationships and behaviors within a model, context or scenario.
4. **Intelligence** is the ability to learn facts and skills and apply them, especially when this ability is highly developed.
5. **Ideation,** or idea generation, is the process of creating new ideas or concepts. In an organized approach, ideas are generated from the information presented from intelligence gathering and governed by our insights into how these ideas can solve problems or capitalize on opportunities.
6. **Ingenuity** refers to the process of applying ideas to solve problems or meet challenges. Ingenuity leads to invention, design, or configuration of a device or process that adds value to consumers or constituents.
7. **Invention** is the process of creating something new by using creativity or imagination in the design, configuration of a device or process that adds value to consumers or constituents.

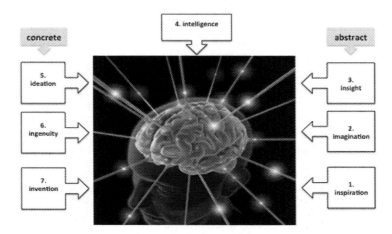

The 7 I's of Creative Intelligence

Figure 3-1: The Seven I's of Creative Intelligence have both abstract and concrete elements.

1. Inspiration

Inspiration is the stimulation for the human mind to produce creative thought. Every human has an innate ability to imagine, but there must be a stimulus. Even subconscious imagination in the form of dreams is caused by some stimulus from thoughts that were formed or influenced by the external environment. A famous moment of environmental inspiration in history was the falling apple that inspired Newton's theories of gravity.

Inspiration can come from messages processed through your five senses: sight, smell, touch, hearing and taste. Because these five senses are constantly in use, there must be particular attention paid to special stimulus that can inspire our creativity. People who are able to process special stimuli from their environment have heightened imaginations. We often refer to this as having an overactive imagination. Actually it is a heightened awareness to infinite stimulus around us. Because there are so many stimuli we construct filters and barriers. That is why we have to sometimes "stop and smell the flowers." The flowers have always been there but we have to make a special effort sometimes to pay attention.

In an article entitled "The Neuroscience of Leadership," authors Rock and Schwartz discuss some of the cognitive barriers to creativity in terms of organizational change. [33] Using magnetic resonance imaging (MRI) technologies their neuroscience research indicates humans are predisposed to resist change, which can be a major inhibiting factor for creativity. Their cognitive theories about the physiological nature of the brain suggest an important technique for improving creativity is focused attention. Attention is the cognitive process of selectively concentrating on one thing while ignoring other things. Focused attention is the ability to respond discretely to specific visual, auditory, or tactile stimuli.

This neuroscience research suggests the brain is a quantum environment with characteristics similar to the quantum zeno effect in physics, which theorizes that the rate of observation has measurable effects on the phenomenon being observed. Similarly, in neuroscience the mental act of focusing attention on new information allows the brain to make neuron connections and keeps synapse circuitry open and dynamically alive. This focused attention eventually causes chemical links and physical changes in the structure of the brain thereby reshaping the patterns of the brain. Consequently, efficient creativity must take into account how to intentionally inspire human imagination by focusing attention on new stimuli.

2. Imagination

When the mind is adequately inspired, the human imagination can become more disciplined and intentional. Imagination must be put into context for humans to understand the meaning of the images produced from thought. Without context it reminds me of a line from an old Temptations song, "It was just my imagination, running away with me."

Disciplined and intentional imagination is at the root of creativity. Understanding these nuisances of imagination is critical to ensuring our efforts of creativity are purposeful and focused. Stimulating imagination by getting people to pay sufficient attention to new ideas should lead to a more innovative mind.

The human mind has built-in simplification mechanisms such as mental schemas, biases and self-deception. These filters in the cognitive system are useful features that allow the human mind to concentrate on the task at hand and not get overwhelmed by an infinite amount of data. Systems that enhance disciplined imagination can be useful for realizing the human potential for creativity. One key factor is a person's ability to think in unconventional ways, understand which ideas are worth pursuing, articulate those ideas and convince others of the value of the ideas.

There are many barriers to creativity that inhibit disciplined imagination. For humans, change is unexpectedly difficult because it provokes physiological discomfort. Preconceptions have a significant impact on what people perceive.

The previously mentioned neuroscience research also discusses attention density, which is focused attention that is purposeful and repeated. It allows humans to overcome their resistance to change and can lead to long-lasting personal evolution. However, when the brain perceives differences between expectations and actuality it treats it as an error, often reacting in the part of the brain's fear circuitry with a fear or anger response. This draws energy from the part of the brain that supports higher intellectual functions. Furthermore, changing routine behavior can overpower rational thought, as well as amplify stress and discomfort.

In their conclusions Rock and Schwartz offer some observations related to what works and what doesn't in terms of overcoming these barriers:

- The conventional empathic approach of getting people on board by establishing trust and rapport through connection and persuasion doesn't sufficiently engage people.
- Change efforts based on incentive and threat rarely succeed in the long run.
- From an organizational perspective, this resistance to change often manifests as a silo mentality.

3. **Insight**

Insight, the ability to understand or the process of "sense-making," is a critical step in the creative process. Insight allows us to make sense of images and thoughts produced by our imagination. This key perspective of creativity centers on how the human mind goes through the process of ideation in order to gain insight.

Rock and Schwartz also suggest some of the following activities in order for us to cultivate moments of insight, as part of a more disciplined and reliable creative process, which are strong enough to change mental maps:

- Create an event or experience that allows people to provoke themselves, to change attitudes and expectations.
- Achieve attention density by concentrating on a specific idea or mental experience.
- Make a deliberate effort to hardwire the brain by paying repeated attention to a mental construct.
- Create a replicable process to stimulate a complex set of new connections that has the potential to enhance our mental resources and overcome brain's resistance to change.

Insights must be generated from within. People will experience an adrenaline-like rush of insight only if they go through the process of making connections themselves. Similar to a nuclear physics particle reactor, gamma rays (low levels, of course) are produced in the brain at the moment of insight.

These neural networks are invariably influenced by experiences and patterns of attention. Graphic visualization is a useful way to focus attention and help humans achieve attention density. These techniques help to visualize the organization's environment, strategic goals and operational issues. They also help create a knowledge management infrastructure for research input. Visualization techniques facilitate the creation and communication of knowledge and build task consensus through the use of computer and non-computer-based, complementary, graphic representation techniques.

One such visualization technique is called "visualization prototyping." Visualization prototyping uses a mind map, which is a diagram used to represent words, ideas, tasks, or other items linked to and arranged radially around a central key word or idea. It is used to generate, visualize, structure and classify ideas, and as an aid in studying, organizing, problem-solving, decision making and writing.

Mind mapping software is a very popular computer-based method for achieving a visualization prototype. It is good for capturing linear thinking models, but is limited to associative logic. For example, we use the visual of the honeycomb structure to illustrate an interactive environment that accommodates a more emergent mental process that iteratively considers a nearly infinite number of permutations from the intersections of thoughts, ideas, and information.

4. Intelligence

Intelligence is the ability to process discrete information after insight has provided context. Intelligence enables humans to define, gather, analyze, and interpret information into a usable format. There are four basic types: active, strategic, open, and organization intelligence. Their use depends on the type of information being processed for sense-making.

Active intelligence refers to information that is relevant to current plans and decisions. The value of strategic intelligence is determined by its ability to help predict the future. Planning activities such as foresight visioning and long-term planning is improved by strategic intelligence. Open intelligence refers to processing information that is publicly available. This contrasts with information on competitors that may be secret or at least covertly obtained. Organization intelligence is the capability of an organization to make sense of information pertinent to its business.

5. Ideation

Ideation is the process of using your imagination, insight, and intelligence to create new thoughts that will translate into tangible outcomes. It is the point where creativity transforms into the conceptual stage of new strategies, products, or policy. Linear thinking has been a very traditional approach using associative logic. More system thinking approaches include metaphoric, divergent, and convergent thinking.

Linear thinking is a process of thought following a step-by-step progression in a determined sequential path. The linear thinking model depends on being able to associate a thought with something that has already been processed in the mind. When we use associative logic we look for similarities rather than something new. This approach is inherently limited by previous experiences and the ability to find common patterns rooted in the past.

For example, intelligence quotient (IQ) tests employ the technique of determining what is similar in a picture. Or how many times have you offered a totally new idea, only to have someone say, "oh, is it like…?" It is human nature to filter new information through our internal database to see if it can be catalogued based on old information and experiences. Because of the limits of associative thinking we tend to share what we already know. Data used in this thinking model are historical, not future-focused, such as reports on the current state of technology rather than anticipating technology trajectories or potential disruptive future technology.

Ideation based on associative thinking uses common techniques such as surveys, focus groups and suggestion boxes. A survey has built-in associative logic in how it is organized. Questions are designed to elicit opinions and evaluate established ideas, activities or products. A more interactive version of surveys is focus groups, in which a group leader uses open-ended questions to obtain feedback on the established paradigm. Feedback prioritizes current knowledge for the purpose of evaluation. The suggestion box, pioneered by National Cash Register in 1895, is a more unstructured, individualized and random approach to ideation.

Linear thinking is often manifested as a "silo mentality". The silo is a comfort zone fortified with old information that has been pasteurized to eliminate risk. Other members of the silo justify the existing paradigm in a broad groupthink. Basically it is too hard and too risky to venture out of the silo and take on innovation as a normal practice. Connecting these silos of thought requires a high level of systems thinking.

Systems thinking is a way of breaking out of these logical constraints. This approach recognizes many factors may combine in complex ways to create sometime surprising futures (due to non-linear feedback loops). It also allows the inclusion of factors difficult to formalize, such as novel insights about the future, deep shifts in values and unprecedented regulations or inventions.

Metaphoric thinking incorporates an analogical process of cross-domain or cross-experience mapping to express or understand an unfamiliar concept. One technique is to explore parallels with some other experience and find metaphors to express these similarities:

1. Conceptualize the problem.
2. Search for prior experiences or proximal experiences.
3. Select and test an analog.
4. Develop an analogy.
5. Seek insights from the exercise.

Thinkers typically use past experiences to derive common characteristics in the problem conceptualization phase. This involves both deductive and inductive processes. Deductively, if the object is something like the source, and if source has quality x, then target may have quality x. At the same time, the process is inductive because it involves extrapolation from the knowledge base. But as with linear thinking, the thinker is limited by past experiences to find parallel metaphors.

Divergent thinking is used in the creativity process to expand or broaden views; the approach focuses first on making sense of the problem, rather than immediately seeking a solution to a problem that is not well understood. Identifying elements relevant to the discussion question is one of the earliest divergent activities related to the *sense-making* phase of brainstorming.

Unfortunately, well-intentioned processes, based on divergent thinking associated with outside the box thinking, often leave you so far outside the existing paradigm that they go beyond what is feasible or possible. For example, De Bono's Six Hat approach is intended to create isolated, yet provocative statements.[34]

Convergent thinking applies standard knowledge in an attempt to narrow the focus and build consensus on a small number of decisions. A popular convergent approach to ideation is scenario analysis and development. Shell Oil, a pioneer in this area more than three decades ago, started by building half a dozen or more scenarios. But they found their managers selected just one of these to concentrate on. As a result the planners reduced the number to three, which managers could handle easily and that is the typical number for scenario analyses today. Using systems thinking in conjunction with scenario planning can lead to plausible scenario story lines because the causal relationship between factors can be demonstrated. The problem with this approach is that it assumes that these three ideas are the best. This methodology does not lend itself to exploring the nearly infinite possibilities.

Brainstorming and Brainwriting: Emergent idea creation is an important function in organizations for stimulating innovation. Idea creation is often accomplished through group activities such as brainstorming and an individual process called brainwriting. Brainstorming is a decision making technique used to describe the verbal generation of ideas by a group. Some research suggests that brainstorming is 44 percent more effective than traditional problem solving methods.[35]

In contrast, brainwriting emphasizes the silent generation of ideas in writing, which are then shared with the group to invigorate new ideas. Brainwriting will produce more ideas than brainstorming, although not necessarily more unique or better quality. The quality of creative and innovative ideas using brainwriting depends on the idea exchange process. Input also can improve by alternating between nominal (individual) and verbal (group) environments. This may be attributed to the fact that while some participants have concerns about oral expression in front of groups, others have difficulty expressing ideas in writing. The ideation process can be enhanced using computer based systems, such as group support systems and electronic brainstorming systems, which I discuss in more detail in Chapter 6.

Some organizations have used electronic versions of suggestion boxes as a pretense for an advanced form of ideation. These Electronic Brainstorming Systems (EBS) generally store and share the ideas but do little to help stimulate novel ideas. Instead, decision making takes the form of evangelizing pet projects or ideas in which we have a vested interested in succeeding. Worse yet, we tend to regress to ideas that don't exceed our comfort zone or don't involve major risk. Because our vision is limited by current expertise we often miss the possibilities. As a result, we often implement the familiar. Connecting these silos of thought requires a high level of systems thinking that we offer in our 6 Step Collective Intelligence™ methodology (see Chapter 5).

6. **Ingenuity**

Ingenuity is the process of inventing something new and tangible. This basically means taking a concept, image, or thought and creating something tangible such as a product, service, program or policy. In an organization this is often the domain of the engineer. In many cases a design or concept is handed off from the scientist in the lab or the design team. It becomes the engineer's job to make something that functions optimally based on the designer's concept.

But human ingenuity can also be seen in the development of new social organizations, institutions and relationships. Ingenuity involves the most complex human thought processes, bringing together our thinking and acting both individually and collectively to take advantage of opportunities or to overcome problems.

The context of the problem is obviously a critical element in how we consider a range of possible solutions. The available possibilities must be considered before we proceed with some course of action. Ingenuity involves all of the dimensions of human cognition mentioned before including disciplined imagination, insight, and inspiration.

Barriers to ingenuity can be crippling as well. Applying outdated paradigms of form, fit and function may inhibit ingenuity. Sometimes the engineer is not very connected to the needs and interest of the consumer or changing market conditions. The introduction of new information from other knowledge domains may be liberating to the ideation process. Getting people involved from other disciplines is a critical element to making sure ingenuity is addressing the future needs of your target market.

7. Invention

Invention is the outcome of the application of ingenuity to create a new device or process. When an invention is a response to a problem, there is more likelihood that it can create the value that is required for innovation. One thought leader on LinkedIn's "Front End of Innovation" blog described innovation as the combination of invention and exploitation.

How many times have you heard someone say that they originally came up with a great product idea that is now being marketing successfully? Unless they had taken advantage of it and commercialized it, someone else seized the opportunity and created value. Invention leads to innovation once it is transformed into a value proposition.

The Creativity Paradox

Although many CEOs say creative leadership is an important core competency for their employees, a Cornell University research report suggests that it may be counterproductive to reaching senior leadership positions. Three separate studies suggest that when people voice creative ideas, others view them as having less leadership potential.[36] Their conclusion is that creative people are getting filtered out on their way to the top.

What is the reason for this apparent paradox? Evidently our deeply held expectations of creative people and effective leaders are inconsistent. Creative people are viewed as risky and unpredictable. Leaders are expected to reduce uncertainty and champion the norms of the group. We say we want creativity, but what we often want is to preserve the status quo with conformist thinking.

In fact, many of the 1,500 leaders surveyed in 2010 by IBM's Institute for Business Value doubted their abilities to lead through complex times. They are promoted on the unspoken promise to preserve the status quo, but are expected to change the status quo when they reach the top. The bias against selecting the most creative thinkers for the highest jobs was consistent through each of these studies.[37] The study creates a dilemma for developing creative leadership at various levels and roles of the organization:

- Top management team
- Project team leader
- Thought leaders
- Change agents

Develop Creative Leadership

To reach beyond this creativity paradox and become an effective leader it is important to transform your creative intelligence into the practical skills of an Innovation Strategist. Effective leaders are differentiated by their ability to create a vision and inspire people to follow it.

The appropriate leadership style is needed for different types of strategic transformation efforts. Creative leadership is likely to be more appropriate for opportunity recognition activities such as strategic foresight, product development and strategic planning, as described in Chapter 2. These activities require risk-taking, experimentation, change, and challenge to the status quo which creative leadership encourages.

Assess Your Innovation Stakeholder's Style

Innovation starts with people that nurture their creative intelligence and have a passion for excellence. But how do we identify, empower, and connect creative people to ensure collaboration? As the Innovation Strategist you will be called upon to facilitate strategic planning retreats or innovation brainstorming workshops for your client or organization. To initiate the process you should conduct an assessment of your stakeholder's innovation style before or at the beginning of the workshop. First, this assessment will help you identify the innovation styles of your participants so you can ensure diversity of skills and problem solving approaches. Second, it can be useful as an ice-breaker to facilitate the introduction and socialization of group members. If management is successful in coordinating these styles, tremendous innovation breakthroughs are possible.

A popular assessment tool is the Kirston Adaptive and Innovation (KAI) model, a 32-item measure based on three factors: sufficiency vs. proliferation of originality, efficiency, and rule conformity. Kirston proposed that creative styles form a continuum from the most adaptive (implying a preference for solving problems through incremental improvement within the system) to the most innovative (preference for restructuring the system in order to solve the problem).

Studies of mid-career MBA students in the United Kingdom, Australia and the United States indicate that members of the more externally oriented managerial functions (such as marketing and strategic planning) score more innovatively than more internally oriented managers (such as in production management, accounting and quality control). However, within each of the major functional areas of management, relatively internally oriented and relatively externally oriented management groups can be identified; moreover, the latter score significantly more innovatively than the former.

The authors apply the relevance of these findings to the management of change in organizations and for the composition and management of effective task groups. This is especially important in view of recent claims that all managers must embrace and cope with "radical and turbulent" change.[38] However, this two-dimensional scale is somewhat limited in describing how human capital can be developed for organizational creativity.

Another instrument, called the "Innovation Styles© assessment," measures typical approaches to problem solving and idea creation. The model has eight innovation profiles that are variations of the four descriptions of how innovation styles are manifested—visioning, experimenting, exploring, and modifying:[39]

Visioning

- Providing "the big picture" and long-term direction
- Focusing on a vision/goal even though the path to get there is uncertain

Experimenting

- Providing methods/systems to take risk in stages (for example, with a good research design) even when the outcome/goal is uncertain
- Getting people to collaborate, be involved in decision-making, and developing a process for planning and working together

Exploring

- Challenging accepted ways of seeing things and seeking out novel approaches to problems
- Dealing with turbulent change through a sense of courage or adventure

Modifying

- Keeping change relevant to current needs
- Responding to immediate needs and maximizing available resources
- Helping short-term motivation by finding practical ways to get immediate "successes"

Our Collective Intelligence methodology uses six profiles of the eight profiles of the Innovation Styles assessment tool and applies an ecosystem label to the behavior to provide a more colorful descriptor as listed and described below:

1. Visionary (Radiator)
2. Visionary/explorer (Rainmaker)
3. Explorer (Pollinator)
4. Explorer/experimenter (Harvester)
5. Experimenter (Landscaper)
6. Modifier (Cultivator)

Using our ecosystem metaphor, each of these profiles is described in terms of their impact and role in developing a system of innovation.

- **Radiator:** Radiators are visionary leaders provide "sunlight" for the organization. This profile is similar to the "charismatic leader". They radiate the energy that catalyzes the transformation effort just as photosynthesis converts energy from the sun into elements of growth for plant life. Steve Jobs and Jake Welch are iconic examples of this profile.

- **Rainmaker:** Water is another critical element for a thriving ecosystem, carrying the nutrients necessary for growth. In the business ecosystem it can originate from the top of the organization as precipitation or from below as irrigation. Rainmakers are individuals who make things happen. Many times the innovation outside the scientific departments happens with top executives who are visionaries and rainmakers. But as in the natural ecosystem, not all rain reaches the ground. If the environment is a "dry desert" and they have not taken to time to develop and cultivate the environment for innovation, rainmakers will not realize their growth potential and their results will be sub-optimal. You can make an argument that Bill Gates of Microsoft, Jeffrey Immelt of General Electric and Michael Eisner of Disney fit this profile.

- **Pollinator:** Pollinators are the innovation stakeholders considered to be thought leaders in the organization. They typically engage other departments with ideas and facilitate cross-fertilization of ideas and multi-functional activities. This activity can be seen in nature by bees pollinating flowers. Pollinators exhibit the characteristics of the explorer style. Clayton Christensen has evolved as the premier thought leader in innovation with a series of books that have cross-pollinated ideas on disruptive innovation between the commercial, healthcare, and education sectors.

- **Harvester:** Harvesters take an idea and develop it into a viable product, service, or market just like the harvester in agriculture gathers mature crops from the fields. They exhibit traits of an entrepreneur and intrapreneur and fit the explorer/experimenter style. Ted Turner pioneered television journalism with the creation of global 24/7 news reporting on CNN. Mark Zuckerberg, the Facebook creator has revolutionized how we interact with each other in a flash of brilliance born out of emotional rejection in his Harvard dorm room.

- **Landscaper:** Landscapers perform the design function of the ecosystem, similar to how landscape architects design plantings and green spaces. They use their knowledge of the subject matter and environment to evaluate, organize and plan the strategic initiative. In the innovation styles model, the landscaper closely resembles the profile of the experimenter and often takes on the role of project manager.
- **Cultivator:** The cultivator performs the analysis and research activities, providing knowledge, scientific inquiry and research-based validation for innovation efforts. The cultivator closely resembles the modifier style.

By way of an example of the Innovation Styles© assessment tool, I have provided my personal report. My dominant innovation style is that of Explorer, followed closely by Visionary (see Figure 3-2). This suggests that I typically behave as a rainmaker who challenges existing paradigms by providing a view of the "big picture".

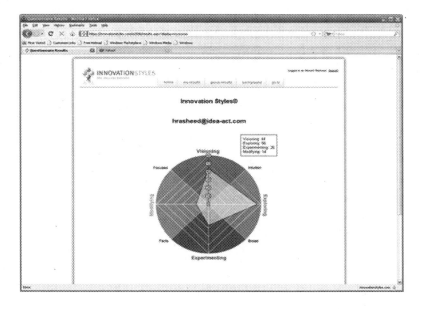

Figure 3-2. My dominant innovation style is that of explorer, followed closely by visionary.

Innovation styles can apply to internal or external stakeholders. For example, the extreme experimenter resembles the activities of an outside consultant or facilitator. The experimenter can represent the internal project leader.

The innovation style assessment is a valuable tool that lends perspective on how we process information and, consequently, helps us understand ourselves. It allows the Innovation Strategist to create better teams in organizations so there will be a diversity of approaches and maximize potential. Innovation stakeholders can complete an online assessment of their innovation style when engaging in a group innovation activity, such as a strategic retreat. A graph included in the assessment of each group profile can help determine the optimum mix of styles for the team, based on the type of project. Beginning a project with this tool as described in the following Call to Action facilitates team building and, ultimately, the free flow of ideas as groups embrace the diversity of problem-solving styles.

Call to Action

Assess you Innovation Stakeholders

1. Make a list of the innovation stakeholders in your value network. Be sure to include external stakeholders such as customers, suppliers and investors.
2. Have each stakeholder complete the innovation style online assessment.
3. Assign groups based on as much profile diversity as possible.
4. Have your innovation team identify the roles of each. Some may have multiple roles, depending on the stage of the process.
5. Discuss how to empower them through better communication, tools and facilitation.

Marching to a Different Beat

An article published by the United States Army, "Adapt or Die: The Imperative for a Culture of Innovation in the U.S. Army," discusses the mindset of the service as a limiting factor for an innovation culture.[40] In part, the article states:

"Our customers are more focused on the optimization of their current capabilities as a hedge against today's potential crises, rather than on how the force will look and operate in 20 years. To change their culture they maintained that they must change behavior. One of the critical behavioral changes relates to experimentation."

It continues, "Our concepts of development and experimentation plan, rather than seeking to confirm or deny a singular hypothesis, would seek to determine the relative merits of several alternative solutions."

In the conclusion the article recommends focusing on the following in order to spur innovation:

- Teaming behavior that is cross-functional
- Parallel thinking behavior that involves non-institutional groups of experts
- Critical thinking behavior that leaves rank at the door
- Learning organizational behavior
- Thirst for creativity and a hunger for challenge
- Search for best practices
- Historical research
- Communities of practice
- After-action reviews
- Information push
- Engagement of critics
- Open environment

The Qualities of Innovative Stakeholders

What are the qualities of a creative leader? The following traits provide guidance for the Innovation Strategist in your attempts to develop productive innovation stakeholders.[41]

- Innovative people are distinguished by their ability to challenge dogma and accepted ideas, and by their confidence in taking risks. They are inhibited if their work environment makes them fearful of being wrong.
- Innovative people bring new elements together that haven't been combined before. This is less about coming up with "odd ideas" and more about responding creatively to a perceived need or problem.
- Innovative people are energized by the prospect of coming up with solutions that are meaningful, relevant and workable. This is not about coming up with new ideas for their own sake.
- Innovative people are "hyper-responsive" to their external environment. They respond to hard problems or challenges with more insightful and illuminating solutions than their "non-innovative" peers.
- In order to have a thriving innovation culture people in organizations must sense there is a need for change and that there is space to explore, experiment and fail. The pressure to innovate must be embedded in "organizational DNA."
- Innovation stakeholders must feel empowered to take responsibility for their own job descriptions, and harness the potential of their learning communities to create the interactions necessary for innovation.

Innovation Management

Managing innovative organizations may be more challenging than leading them. The diffusion of knowledge and the harnessing of learning communities will require very different management skills. It requires creating the right environment for innovation. While requiring a lot of teacher-student contact and is resource-intensive, innovation skills can be taught.[42]

Successful management of innovative people recognizes the following truths about innovative people:

- They have multiple professional identities and belong to many professional communities, networks and teams.
- They thrive on exchanging knowledge and problem solving across "porous" organizational boundaries and in flatter, less hierarchical and more supportive structures.
- They are highly mobile within their learning communities and should be encouraged to network and collaborate.

Innovation Incentives

A key element of any innovation system is how to reward stakeholders. The concept of "experiential capitalism" explains how innovative people are driven primarily by the personal satisfaction of what they do. [43]

Innovative people are not motivated by financial rewards. They respond better to self and peer appraisal than to hierarchical performance management systems. They are motivated by the quality of work they are given and rewarded by the allocation of projects. They tend to work in bursts of activity and may need to be given "space" to recover.

External elements, such as networks and learning communities, also contribute to a viable innovation culture. Innovative organizations understand the importance of investing in "network capital." They encourage innovative people to attend conferences, exchange knowledge internally and externally, and move on in their careers, knowing that when they leave they remain in their learning communities.

Leaders must accept that the only way to understand one of the risks associated with innovation is to fail. They must modify their performance management systems to avoid encouraging innovative people to seek "safe ground." Organizational accounting systems must value intangibles. The uncertainty of innovation, including managing its risks and costs, must be reflected in the skill sets of accountants. Performance management systems within organizations must avoid dis-incentivizing innovative behavior[44].

Innovation Coaching

Innovation coaching can stimulate the leadership thinking processes and provide a mechanism for leaders to practice innovative leadership. The International Coach Federation defines coaching as partnering with clients in a thought-provoking and creative process that inspires them to maximize their personal and professional potential.

Business coaching is the practice of providing positive support and positive feedback while offering occasional advice to an individual or group to help them recognize how to improve the effectiveness of their business. To inspire innovation stakeholders in an organization and help develop innovative human capital, coaching after training is an effective approach.

PART II

Strategies for Sustainable Innovation

CHAPTER 4

CREATE A SUSTAINABLE BUSINESS MODEL: KEY #4

No one can possibly achieve any real and lasting success or "get rich" in business by being a conformist.—J. Paul Getty

Business Models: The New Frontier of Value Creation

Even as recently as a decade ago, who could have anticipated that you could rent cars by the hour 24/7, play a real-time video game with other enthusiasts from around the world, or have your own personal radio station with tunes from your favorite recording artists? Groupon is not your grandmother's version of clipping coupons. Their initial public offering at $18 billion is based on a business model innovation that has made potential competitors salivate. But their $430 million annual loss in 2011 has made it questionable whether it is sustainable or just a passing fad.

These are just a sampling of the new business models that have emerged that are changing our everyday life. You can be sure the future will be full of interesting new disruptions. Are you ready to be a non-conformist and proactively find new opportunities to create disruptions in your industry? The fourth key is to create a sustainable business model.

Just as technological innovation can be radical or incremental, the business model can be as well. It could be a major disruption of the standard value proposition of the industry, causing a shift in markets, infrastructure, cost efficiencies and revenue streams. Or it could be a business model "pivot," a minor shift affecting only certain aspects of the firm's way of doing business?

Business Model Innovation (BMI) has become the new frontier of value creation. In a 2005 survey by The Economist Intelligence Unit, more than 50 percent of executives had predicted that BMI would be even more important for success than product or service innovation by 2010. [45] Similarly, in a 2008 IBM survey, nearly all CEOs polled reported the need to adapt their business models, with more than two-thirds saying that extensive changes were needed.[46] However, according to a recent American Management Association study, no more than 10 percent of innovation investment at global companies is focused on developing new business models.[47] That translates into a large gap and huge potential for innovation.

Just how important business model innovation has become is obvious from the following fact:

Between 1997 and 2007, 14 of the 19 entrants into the Fortune 500 achieved significant success because their business model innovations have transformed existing industries or created new ones.[48]

Business model innovation can involve creating a new business model or reinventing your existing business model. New business models are necessary for exploiting new technologies, or new strategies at the corporate, competitive or functional level. For example, companies looking to execute a growth strategy through diversification can use the business model innovation process to consider its feasibility.

Is Your Business Model Still Relevant?

With the frequent seismic shifts in our new global economy organizations must continually question whether their existing business model is still relevant. A major disruption caused by the introduction of new technology or a new value proposition from competitive differentiation may cause a shift in the dominant industry business model. Shifts in costs and pricing structures, changes in the infrastructure, human resources, or core competencies in the marketplace may cause disruptions that require firms to reinvent their existing business model. Target market repositioning or re-branding may be required if consumer needs or demographic profiles shift.

The Business Model Innovation framework provides a structured approach to determine whether a minor shift or whether a total reinvention is required to generate profitable growth. The term business model describes informal and formal core aspects of a business. It is the conceptual and architectural implementation of a business strategy and the foundation for the implementation of business processes.

In his book *Business Model Generation,* Alex Osterwalder proposed a business model design composed of four main pillars: product innovation, infrastructure management, customer relationship and financial aspects.[49] Visualizing the business model as an architectural structure suggests each component is compartmentalized. Rather than compartmentalizing a business model, like rooms in a house, an organic metaphor suggests a more dynamic flow of energy among components that can be visualized from a cellular perspective.

Cellular Business Model Innovation

I like to use an ecosystem metaphor to illustrate the interdependencies of elements that enable renewable and sustainable innovation at the business model level. This metaphor, which provides perspective on how continuous renewal of your business model can lead to sustainable prosperity, takes into account the complexities that exist in the environment at all levels, from global to micro. As such, a business model ecosystem can be considered an emergent, complex and dynamic system of multi functional and multi level interactions of activities and resources.

A good example of an ecosystem infrastructure is the honeycomb (see Figure 4-1), described as a perfect structure in nature. Contrary to popular belief, the honeycomb is not an octagonal shape. It is a ten-sided structure that maximizes the number of contact points. The honeycomb's permeable structure maximizes the flow of material and energy critical to development and growth.

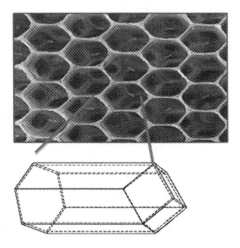

Figure 4-1. The honeycomb provides a good example of an ecosystem infrastructure.

The permeability of the honeycomb cell is a great metaphor for the efficient diffusion of knowledge needed in an organization. Rather than depending on the goodwill and cooperation of a single contact point (manager), an innovation system with semi-permeable boundaries that facilitate diffusion of a diverse and unfiltered flow of information will accelerate innovation. The greater the diversity of thought, the richer the harvest of ideas can be. The 10 sides demonstrate the importance of sharing knowledge with as many diverse contact points in an organization as possible. Using the cellular perspective the nine components of the business model can be illustrated as interlocking and interdependent cells, each with the potential for value creation.

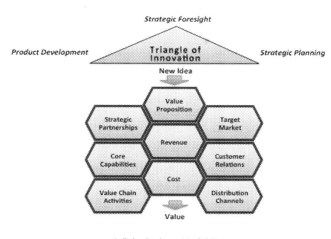

Figure 4-2. As shown above, the business model is the logic behind value creation.

New ideas produced from foresight, planning and product development activity can lead to new value propositions, which are statements of how an organization can resolve constituent problems or satisfy customer needs and generate value. These value propositions can also articulate new ideas from policy initiatives in the macro environment, new and disruptive technology in the industry, or strategic goals of the firm. The input for the business model should be reinvented or reassessed regularly.

Business model innovation results in restating the value proposition and identifying elements in your infrastructure, target markets, and financial model that need to change. Each of the nine components of the business model serves as interdependent cellular elements as pictured in figure 4-3. Similar to the concept of co-evolution in a natural ecosystem, innovation in any subcategory can result in change in another category. Only a three-dimensional model similar to the 10-sided beehive can demonstrate the multi-faceted possibilities for interactive change in a business model ecosystem.

Of course an organization can have multiple business models. Imagine a three dimensional structure of connected value propositions (see figure 4-3). Sharing infrastructure and market functions between multiple product offerings can derive new revenue streams or provide cost efficiencies. Or you can use one product offering to generate multiple revenue sources. You can also use multiple product offerings that share infrastructure such as core capabilities or strategic partners or share distribution channels.

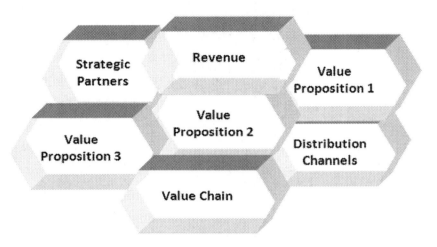

Figure 4-3. Sharing business model functions between product offerings can generate new revenue streams and cost efficiencies.

In other words for each value proposition that represents a different product or service innovation you can share the same trusted strategic partners and/or reliable distribution channels. You can derive cost efficiencies from a well-trained workforce, economies of scale, and learning curve productivity due to familiar value chain functions that are shared between offerings.

According to a McKinsey report, using multisided business models is a new trend that creates value through interactions between multiple players. One example mentioned in the report is how, the media industry, the print media, and the television media offer shared content and generate multiple revenue sources, through third party advertising and consumer based subscriptions. Another example is Spiceworks, which offers information technology services at no charge and generates revenue from advertising from B2B companies that want access to their database of nearly one million users. A third example, Sermo, is a free online community of physicians for networking. It generates revenue from pharmaceutical companies, health care organizations, financial institutions, and government bodies who want access to the anonymous interactions and polls of Sermo's members.[50]

Sustain your Business Model with Intellectual Property

Recent changes in patent laws have made it easier to sustain business model innovation as intellectual property, particularly as business method patents. For many years the U.S. Patent and Trademark Office (USPTO) took the position that "methods of doing business" are not patentable. Despite the emergence of patent applications based on the Internet or computer enabled methods of commerce, USPTO required that business method inventions must advance the "technological arts" in order to be patentable. Its guidelines to examiners required that a process for doing business must produce a concrete, useful and tangible result.

The Leahy-Smith America Invents Act of 2011 is the first significant change in the U.S. patent system in 60 years. Business method patents are now more viable and should be processed faster because of more government resources dedicated to this area and more clarity in administrative instructions to patent examiners.

The following are examples of recent business method patent filings by well-known companies that have been a source of the tremendous growth in value they have experienced:

Amazon

Amazon.com enables customers to purchase books, music, videos and other items over the Internet. To distinguish its shopping experience from the competition, it filed patents on its Internet business methods. The 1-Click ordering was an example of an innovative business method for Internet retail that was not sophisticated and complicated to replicate.

Barnes and Noble introduced a similar concept called Express Lane on its website and set off a firestorm of litigation and reaction from the Internet business community, criticizing the alleged misuse of patent laws. The following demonstrates how Amazon's methods are articulated in patent filings:

- Method and system for placing a purchase order via a communications network (One-click purchase)
- Secure method and system for communicating a list of credit card numbers over a non-secure network
- Secure method for communicating credit card data when placing an order on a non-secure network
- Method and apparatus for structuring the querying and interpretation of semi-structured information
- Method for data gathering around forms and search barriers
- Method for producing sequenced queries
- Internet-based customer referral system (Affiliate program)
- Method and system for conducting a discussion relating to an item

Priceline

Priceline.com was invented to allow sellers of low variable cost, perishable services to clear excess capacity or inventory without undercutting their own retail processes. Its innovative business model, "Name Your Own Price," leverages the Internet to collect brand-flexible demand and deliver it to consumers. Walker Digital, a privately held research and development lab founded by Jay Walker, developed these business method systems. The patent filing listed the following claims:

- Conditional purchase offer buyer agency system
- Conditional purchase offer management system for telephone calls
- Conditional purchase offer management system for event tickets.
- Conditional purchase offer management system for cruises
- Conditional purchase offer management system for collectibles
- Conditional purchase offer management system

- Method and system for utilizing a psychographic questionnaire in a buyer-driven commerce system
- System and method for motivating submission of conditional purchase offers
- Method and apparatus for the sale of airline-specified flight tickets
- Method, apparatus, and program for pricing, selling, and exercising options to purchase airline tickets
- Method and apparatus for a cryptographically assisted commercial network system designed to facilitate buyer-driven conditional purchase offers (with Walker Digital lab)

Google

Google was granted its first patent for a method of determining the relevance of Web pages in relation to search queries in 2003.[51] The patent governs methodology for parsing through Web documents to deliver Web surfers the most relevant pages for their queries using an improved search engine that refines a document's relevance score based on interconnectivity of the document within a set of relevant documents. So, a document with a high interconnectivity with other documents in the initial set of relevant documents would indicate that the document has some level of viability in the set, and therefore the document's ranking will increase. In this manner, the search engine re-ranks the initial set of ranked documents to refine the initial rankings.

This initial patent established Google with a sustainable business model in the search engine industry using a revenue model based on advertising. But subsequent patent filings question whether their future business model is as a smart phone company, a memory module manufacturer or a server maker. The patents acquired by purchase or license include phone related patents from Verizon, patents involving video and streaming data from IBM, as well as other hardware related patents. These patents include intellectual property about self-driving cars. A blogger, Bill Slawki, listed 187 patents granted as of 2009:

- Advertising Patents (61)
- Analytics (7)

- Annotations Patents (1)
- Audio Patents (2)
- Blog Search Patents (1)
- Client/Server Patents (15)
- Database Management Patents (3)
- Design Patents (21)
- Distributed Data Patents (3)
- Document Presentation Patents (1)
- Duplicate Content Patents (14)
- E-commerce Patents (4)
- Email and Messaging Patents (38)
- Event Modeling Patents (3)
- Google Book Patent (13)
- Google Desktop Search Patents (13)
- Google Finance Patents (1)
- Google News Patents (2)
- Google TV Patents (3)
- Handwriting Analysis Patents (2)
- Hardware Patents (57)
- Image and Video Patents (80)
- Intellectual Property Patents (2)
- Language Conversion Patents (1)
- Large File Space Indexing Patents (34)
- Medical Patents (1)
- Modeling and Mapping Patents (37)
- Multi-Language Patents (7)
- Network Patents (15)
- Organizational Communications Patents (2)
- Personal Data Patents (4)
- Personalized Homepage Patent (3)
- Personalized Search Patents (11)
- Phrase-Based Indexing Patents (13)
- Radio Patents (11)
- Reviews and Recommendations Patents (5)
- RSS Patents (2)
- Search Display Patents (30)
- Search Indexing Patents (118)
- Security Patents (5)

- Segmentation Patents (3)
- Shopping Search Patents (3)
- Social Networking Patents (110)
- Software Patents (3)
- Vehicle Patents (11)
- Virtual Machine Task Management Patents (1)
- Visual Modeling (1)
- Voice Search Patents (4)
- Web Authoring Patents (5)
- Web Spam Patents (2)
- Weight Loss Patents (1)
- Wireless and Mobile/Phone Patents (118)

Based on this extensive list, it is hard to determine in which direction Google's business model will evolve and how it will reinvent itself beyond being a search engine company. But it should give some insight to Innovation Strategists where Google sees opportunity in the future. Based on this list, search engine algorithms and mobile devices are apparently the primary business models Google expects to use to sustain it competitive advantage.

The long list of patents by Google over the past 10 years highlights one of the concerns of the small business community. Because the new patent laws favor the first to file, there is a concern that small firms will not have the resources to compete in a highly competitive environment to capitalize on first mover advantages to sustain business models and erect barriers to entry for competitors.

In order to address this potential challenge for small business the U.S. Department of Commerce has initiated a number of programs to educate small business owners using intellectual property workshops and resources that fund the Small Business Innovation grants.

Walmart: The Giant Retail Disruptor

Using business model innovation, entire industries recently have redistributed billions of dollars of value. Retail discounters such as Walmart and Target created disruption by differentiating themselves as low cost retailers with very strong logistic infrastructure and branding, respectively. As of 2009, Walmart and Target accounted for 75 percent of the total valuation of the retail sector. After Walmart introduced its Neighborhood Market concept in 1998 by building supercenters, it quickly became the biggest food retailer in the U.S. Before the domination of Walmart superstores, the supermarket industry market share of the retail grocery business was 90 percent in the late 1980's. The top four companies represented only 34% as of 2010.

How has the competition responded to this disruption over the last 10 years? Some incumbents like Albertson have been cost cutting, reducing administrative and purchasing expenses. Others like Giant Eagle, the largest closely held supermarket company, attempted to reinvent its business model. It rebranded four of its stores as Market District, in an attempt to attract upscale shoppers. It opened Giant Eagle Express and opened Valu King Supermarket as a discount food store, as well as a discount pharmacy. These stores offer free Wi-Fi, churrasco-style foods, a kosher deli, cheese cave and a smoothie bar, an in-store bakery, a full range butcher shop, and a limited deli.

There have been other innovative responses to the dominance of Walmart. For example, a utility patent was filed in 2006 for a retail shopping system to support a franchise of small retail merchant operators of perishable goods, non-perishable goods, and operators of service trades. Franchisees are co-located in a common building and supported by a common grocery retail system. In this innovation, the franchiser provides property rights to the franchisee, which include patents, trademarks, copyrights, know-how, trade secrets, leases, branding, advertising, training, front-end operations, merchant member business services, business support programs, Internet data bases and marketing services, banking services, payroll services, employee health and medical benefits services.

As a result of competitors copying their productivity methods and dollar stores penetrating the urban markets, Walmart market share declined for the first time in 2010. Now Walmart is considering reinventing its business model. It is experimenting with smaller Neighborhood Markets and Marketside stores to penetrate markets in which it faced resistance by community groups because of perceptions it is unfair to workers and other neighborhood stores.

One lesson from history is that although Walmart is king of the hill now, competitors are working hard to disrupt the industry. Just ask the executives at Sears, which used to be the retail monarch. Remember Woolworth? At one time they were the leading music retailer in the United Kingdom. They failed to adjust their business model with the creative disruption of super stores, mall food courts, and iTunes.

So who is next? Google? eBay? Amazon is already making inroads into eBay's intermediary market of online auctions. Regardless of your success, failure to reinvent your business model in the face of disruptions can lead to serious declines in market share and viability.

New Disruptive Business Models

An upcoming business model innovation for retailers is contactless payment. Waving your smart phone in front of the point of sale terminal as if it were a credit card with an electronic wallet can now make payments. Fast food giant McDonald's now has terminals in Canada that accept MasterCard's Paypass, which can be used with Google Wallet, and Visa's Paywave, which is used with Visa's Digital Wallet. Evolving technology called near field communication (NFC) is the new standard that will improve the security of the radio frequency identification (RFID) that these systems use.

Dwolla has initiated a new business model that directly links banks and moves money between accounts to whomever you want, even Facebook friends who don't have Dwolla accounts. As a result Business Insider has designated it as one of the 20 most innovative companies in 2011. Unlike PayPal and Square, both of which use credit cards for transaction, it bypasses credit cards, avoiding high transaction fees. Dwolla takes 25 cents for every transaction, and is currently processing $30 million to $50 million per month on its platform.[52]

The newer payment technologies are far more convenient, but have prohibitive costs that have slowed market penetration. These systems also involve consumer loyalty. One very recent patent involves a configuration system composed of a secure online payment system, an advertising system, and an identity system (patent by Hertel et al., 2011)

Exciting new business models are evolving from the convergence of two or more existing concepts. Zynga, a San Francisco-based social gaming company, capitalized on the convergence of video gaming and social media to create a new market called social gaming, which is taking video gaming viral. Instead of playing with the computer or the person on the couch next to you, you can create and interact with a community of fellow players. This market was made possible because they used Facebook's social media platform, which went from one million users in 2004 to 600 million in 2010.[53] Zynga grossed $850 million in 2010. In fact its 47 percent profit margin, when compared to Google's 29 percent and Apple's at 28 percent, was touted as the most profitable ever by Business Insider. [54]

This is still after Zynga pays royalties in the form of advertising to acquire users and 30 percent of virtual goods sales to Facebook. Zynga's virtual goods product offering is another revenue stream with tremendous profit margins since it does not cost much to produce, nothing to store, and does not need a sales force.

Other emerging business models have captured our imagination, but have yet to capture value in terms of profit. Twitter has engaged more than one billion people around the world. It has helped topple governments in the Arab world and helped destroy political careers in the United States. Twitter, however, has yet to find a way to monetize its viral success. Twitter has difficulty capturing user data that creates value for targeted advertising. Google and Amazon on the other hand, were able to convert user profile data into gold for targeted advertising.

Pandora is an Internet radio program that allows you to create your own radio "stations" based on the specific type of music you like by associating similar artists. Its meteoric rise is also challenged by an inability to monetize its business model. In both cases, they seem to be holding on to the Facebook version of the film *Field of Dreams*: "Build it (a large user database) and they (revenue stream) will come." The potential initial public offering value of Facebook—which is expected to be nearly $100 billion—is a promising sign. In the meantime, Twitter and Pandora's market values are skyrocketing, without a profitable financial model.

Then there is the Zipcar. It offered car sharing to more than 8,000 subscribers in 60 major cities by mid-2011, with an annual subscription and an hourly fee. In Los Angeles, for example, a $50 annual fee allows you to rent a car for $8 an hour on weekdays and $9 an hour on weekends. Many nonprofits are using this business model as a social innovation to benefit the under-resourced that have challenges with access to public transportation. Since there is no dominant technology standard with protected intellectual capital on which to base a sustainable competitive advantage, how will Zipcar respond to the inevitable disruptions in its business model?

Creating Disruption in Your Industry's Business Model

The current state of an industry's business model is driven by several internal and external factors. Technological factors influence the product standards, delivery platforms, utility, and features driving value and competition in the industry. Disruptions in technology also influence branding decisions, customer service and channels of distribution. Additionally, new technology or product introductions will require changes in key business processes, core competencies, and human and organizational capital.

One example of industry standards with significant disruptive technology is the Information and Communication Technology (ICT) sector. ICT standards determine how computers operate and software applications are developed, how digital content is produced, processed, distributed and stored, and how transactions of all types are managed. A trend that is an accelerant for disruption to information technology are standards that are "open"—that is, not owned or controlled by any one company or entity. The Internet is the ubiquitous open standard that has generated tremendous innovation by forming a common base upon which others can build.

Environmental factors, such as the economy, are drivers for shifting targets of revenue sources and the dynamics of cost efficiencies. Social factors affect the shifts in customer needs and behavior that, in turn, affect target markets, distribution channels and customer relations. Regulatory factors such as new legislation could create a disruption in product standards, customer needs, or cost efficiencies.

Creating disruption in your industry's dominant business model starts with an audit of its generic value proposition. In deciding how to reinvent your industry's value proposition, you can ask questions at the society level based on the standard environmental scanning model, or at an industry level using the "Five Forces Model" popularized by Michael Porter.[55] Answering these questions will facilitate knowledge discovery. The following macro-level questions can determine trends that may provide an opportunity or challenge that will lead to future disruptions in your industry and ideas that can lead to a sustainable business model.

Audit Questions for Current Industry Business Model

1. How are customer needs changing?
2. How are consumer tastes and perceptions changing?
3. How are customer demographics changing?
4. How are social customs changing?
5. How is the economic climate changing?
6. How are the core technologies in the industry changing?
7. How are your competitors developing new products?
8. How is the current competitive strategy effective?
9. How are the barriers to market entry changing?
10. How are your competitors' cost structures changing?
11. What new substitutes are emerging in the marketplace?

This type of audit process provides a systematic approach to environmental scanning process focused on the future. These questions will help focus research on changes in the environment, such as trends in your industry, to discover where potential disruptions may evolve. It will help the Innovation Strategist focus on knowledge that will have an impact on the future to anticipate future opportunities and challenges that may result in shift in the dominant value proposition of the industry.

The link at www.idea-act.com provides a template called the Dynamic Worksheet you can use to research future-focused knowledge that impacts your industry business model. The worksheet is explained in Step 3 of the Six Steps to Collective Intelligence Methodology" in Chapter 5. These templates can be uploaded to the Idea Accelerator database described in Chapter 6 on Collaborative Technology.

Creating Disruption in your Organization's Business Model

Creating disruption in your organization's business model starts by evaluating the current value proposition that articulates how customers are satisfied by current products, services or policies. It describes the way your firm differentiates itself from its competitors and why customers buy from you. Optimally, it should synchronize with the goals of your organization's strategic plan.

Value configuration is the rationale that makes a business mutually beneficial for the organization and its customers based on the following:

- New product or service offering
- New technology or application
- Production efficiency
- Process improvement
- Effective problem solving or customer benefit
- A new technology platform
- A new network affiliate or channel partner
- Software revisions

The value proposition is also a key component of an organization's brand. A clearly articulated value proposition will include some of the following branding variables:

- Corporate slogan
- Products and services
- Product names
- Product features
- Product positioning
- Marketing mixes

The two main components of the value proposition are "the statement of offer" and "the statement of differentiation." The following template can be used to craft a value proposition:

Organization Value Proposition Template

Offer:

For (target customer) _____.

who need _____.

Our (product/service), the _____

provides (benefit(s) _____.

Differentiation:

Unlike our primary competitor(s) _____,

Our product provides the benefits of _____,

as proven by our _____.

I provide an example of how to organize and implement a Business Model Innovation session in the following "Call to Action" guide.

Call to Action

Reinvent your Business Model

Part 1: Business Model Innovation Planning

1. Assess the innovation styles of your participants. Assign roles based on diversity of function and hierarchy for better group dynamics.
2. Build stakeholder consensus on the priority of key and emerging issues in your strategic environment using the following questions.

   • How do we improve performance for our customers?
   • How do we make customization valuable to our customers?
   • How can we provide better accessibility?

- How can we improve the convenience or utility of our products?
- What new product design would our customers value?
- What new branding display would appeal to our customers?
- How can we offer a lower price for the same value?
- How can we reduce our cost?
- How can we reduce our risk?
- How are your profit margins changing?
- What new technology platforms are your competitors developing?
- What new skills are your competitors developing?
- What new strategic alliances are your competitors forming?

Part 2: Business Model Innovation Implementation

1. Assign research tasks to workshop participants to identify trends that provide quantifiable answers to how these dynamics have changed over a period of time (i.e., There has been an X% increase in Y over Z period of time): Use the Dynamic Knowledge Worksheet (see pdf template in Chapter 5) that can be uploaded later into the **Idea Accelerator**™ software.

2. Bring trends to the brainstorming session. Use the Six Step Collective Intelligence system (detailed in Strategy 5) to generate new ideas:

Develop a new value proposition for each of the new ideas or solutions to articulate its value to your existing or new customers.

By way of example, the following is Institute for Innovation's Value Proposition:

The Institute for Innovation Value Proposition

We provide organizations with a sustainable innovation system, collaborative software and consultative support for strategic foresight, development, strategic planning, and business model innovation activities in the commercial, public and social sectors. Our proprietary 6 Step Collective Intelligence process, featuring bisociative brainstorming, accelerates creativity and innovation. The Idea Accelerator software and system "connects the dots from different boxes" to generate new ideas and solutions.

Reinvent Your Organization's Infrastructure

The infrastructure component of the business model includes key value chain activities, core capabilities, and strategic partnerships. Figure 4-4 provides a graphic picture of the typical business infrastructure and each function is discussed in more detail in the following section. The basics of the organization's infrastructure are the same as the value network.

Value Chain activities are the primary functions that your organization engages in to create value for its customers, as depicted by the square boxes in the inner circle. For manufacturers these supply chain functions start with an inbound process of raw materials. For other firms the value chain inbound source could be service clients or data for processing. All firms engage in key processes to add value and outbound these products or services to customers through marketing activities, which are supported by customer service.

Infrastructure

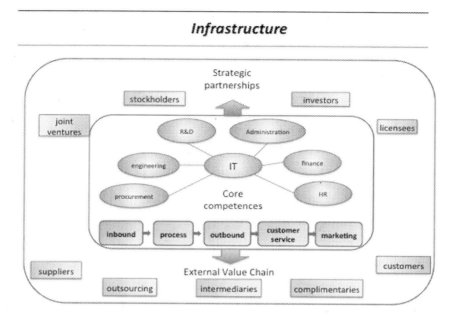

Figure 4-4. The three main components of the infrastructure are the primary and secondary activities (in the inner circle) of the value chain, and the relationships with external stakeholders (outside the circle).

Core capabilities are the internal knowledge, skill, and competencies of the employees inherent in the functional areas, as depicted by the oval shapes in the inner circle (see Figure 4-4). When anticipating a future disruption, you must assess whether it will make your current collective skills and knowledge obsolete or marginally effective. New and disruptive technologies often require new skills, certifications and training. Inaccessibility of talent or cost barriers can inhibit the transformation of an opportunity into a reinvented business model.

Audit Questions for Core Capabilities
1. How are your organization's economies of scale changing?
2. How are your suppliers' cost structures and pricing points changing?
3. How is the availability of supplies changing?
4. What new skills, competencies and certifications do you need to compete in the future?
5. What new equipment do you need to compete in the future?
6. How are your profit margins changing?

Strategic partnerships include the business alliances that complement other aspects of the business model. This includes suppliers and external agencies from which a firm acquires inputs (resources) such as labor, raw material and financial capital. Also, policy makers and legal bodies are influential entities that both set the rules and control the market.

Audit Questions for Strategic Partnerships
What new partnerships and alliances will help your organization:
• Optimize capabilities?
• Achieve economies of scale?
• Reduce risk?
• Acquire key resources?

In order to sustain the infrastructure of your business model you must look for opportunities to develop unique intellectual, human, or social capital that can be patented or branded. A well-designed infrastructure can be achieved by applying innovation processes to each functional relationship. For example building a logistics system that was patentable was how Walmart created a competitive advantage around its low cost business model. Google has made a reputation on hiring the brightest talent and providing an innovative culture that inspires creativity.

Remember that utility patents can provide a means for protecting your intellectual assets that are not your core technology or product design. This could be in the form of process innovation or computer system for support activities. Having strong non-compete and non-disclosure clauses with your strategic partners could deter defections. Incentives to ensure loyalty can keep valuable complementaries who provide ancillary products and intermediaries who distribute products, engaged for mutual benefit.

Also do not forget the ecosystem example of the interdependent beehive. The Innovation Strategist must constantly ask how to create value from the interdependent relationships between internal and external stakeholders that share knowledge and ideas.

The Institute for Innovation Infrastructure

- Our core competence is a patent-pending methodology for harnessing the collective intelligence of your stakeholders. This methodology is leveraged with Idea Accelerator™, a Web 2.0 enterprise level software solution and a mobile application, Trend Search.
- We have an extensive network of Certified Innovation Strategists to provide training and coaching for each of our customer segments.
- The combination of trained people, efficient process and effective technology provides a robust system for reinventing your business model to achieve stakeholder value and profitable growth.

Reinvent your Target Market

Market segmenting is the process of categorizing customers based on similar wants or needs for specific products and services. The market segmentation and branding of the business model should focus on the target audience for a business' products and services. As an Innovation Strategist, you must be able to clearly articulate what industry(s) you are in and the profile of your client, customer or constituents. One approach is to segment the market based on economic sector, industry or type of decision maker:

- Economic Sector: commercial, public, social
- Industry: financial services, manufacturing, consumer goods, etc.
- Decision maker profile: executive, functional-level manager, employee

Market segmentation also matches specific products to consumer profiles that can be classified as:

- Geographic: international, national, regional, and local segments
- Demographic: ethnic, age, gender socio-economic, cultural segments

Finally, market segmentation can be classified by product type and associated buying behavior:

- Psychographic: impulsive v. necessity
- Behavioral: commodity v. premium

Audit Questions for Market Segmentation
1. Which industry segment or sector most values your product offering(s)?
2. Which segment needs does your product offering best satisfy?
3. Which untapped segments hold the greatest potential for disruption?

Distribution Channel is how a company delivers products and services to customers, including the company's marketing and distribution strategy. The distribution channel can be classified as follows:

Organization owned channel

- Direct
- In-house sales force
- Web site
- Stores

Partner-owned channels

- Indirect
- Partner stores
- Wholesaler

Audit Questions for the Distribution Channel
1. Which channels are most cost effective?
2. Which channel is most efficient in reaching your target markets?

Customer relationships are the links a company establishes with its customer segments. The process of managing customer relationships is referred to as customer relationship management (CRM) as listed below:

- Customer acquisition
- Customer retention
- Up-selling
- Personal assistance (travel agencies)
- Self-service (airlines)
- Automated services (airlines)
- Communities (applications and developers, Smartphone)
- Co-creation (Amazon.com reviews)

Social media has evolved as a new and efficient way to develop customer relationships. You can develop customer loyalty programs using Facebook features such as "like" or "share". Consultants now use Linked-in to develop social capital and networks by asking for recommendations and referrals.

Audit Questions for Customer Relationships
1. Which methods of customer relationship management most effectively acquire, satisfy, and retain customer?
2. What new systems are your competitors using to manage customer relationships?

Product or service branding is how an organization creates an identity in the marketplace, articulates its value to customers using symbols and other intangible communication vehicles such as a name, sign, symbol, color combination or slogan. Organizations can create differentiation and sustainable competitive advantage by having a legally protected brand name or trademark. Other types of branding include:

- A **concept brand** is associated with an abstract concept, like breast cancer awareness or environmentalism, rather than a specific product, service or business.
- A **commodity brand** is associated with a commodity. The "Got Milk?" campaign is an example of advertising for a commodity brand.[56]

As mentioned previously the key to sustaining your business model is to develop intellectual property that provides a competitive advantage. In terms of your target market, developing trademarks and branding is essential. Additionally slogans, tags, and customer loyalty programs are critical parts of the branding. Creating loyalty in your distribution channels means creating barriers to exit and high switching cost. Co-marketing, co-branding, retailer support, and loyalty programs are ways to develop and maintain goodwill among your channel partners.

For example, sport leagues such as the National Basketball Association and the National Football League have "official sponsor" campaigns for their loyal advertisers to differentiate them from their competitors. Cisco developed a career development platform called Pipeline and made it accessible for its extensive partner network for critical talent recruitment. Microsoft developed a certification process and designation for its partner network. To be a Microsoft Gold Partner requires certain levels of competencies and a number of projects developed using their software.

Other ways of increasing market development and penetration, improving customer relations, and securing partner relations include:

- Providing exclusive rights, privileges and territories
- Developing cooperative and exclusive use of logos and trademarks
- Sharing CRM systems and customer profile database

The Institute for Innovation Customer Profile

Our primary target markets are:

- Think tanks and development agencies responsible for strategic foresight
- Strategic planning initiatives
- New product development teams
- Technology transfer and commercialization organizations

Our services are delivered using teams of **Certified Innovation Strategists**. Our software is accessible through a web-based subscription model for small organizations or site license for ongoing transformation projects for major organizations.

Reinvent Your Financial Model

The financial, or profit model, includes cost structures and revenue streams. Costs are determined based on the following:

- Cost driven
- Value driven
- Fixed costs
- Variable costs
- Economies of scale

The cost structure is the monetary requirement for acquiring the resources employed in the business model to create value, particularly the direct operating costs. Increasing gross profit margins is obviously a critical success factor for organizations. An organization's infrastructure diagram (figure 4-5) is a good place to analyze cost drivers. For example gross profit is driven by the primary functions and external stakeholder relationships.

Cost Drivers

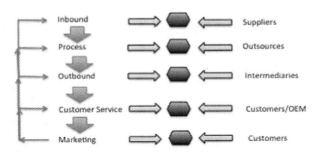

Figure 4-5: Cost drivers are determined by the interactions between primary functions and external relationships.

At each functional intersection between an internal primary activity and external stakeholder relationship there is a cost impact. There are also cost implications between primary and secondary functions such as the relationship between procurement and outsourcing suppliers and between engineering and external R&D labs.

All functional intersections will have some involvement with the information technology department. For example, Enterprise Resource Planning (ERP) software can connect primary function cost drivers with secondary functions such as Accounting, Procurement, and Human Resources. Customer Relations Management (CRM) software can connect primary functions like Marketing and Customer Service with Accounting.

A revenue model describes how organizations create value for themselves by addressing sources of revenue, pricing strategies, and price points. Pricing strategies deal with overall goals, such as "what are we targeting with our offering—high-end versus low-end?"—or "is the offering intended to promote another offering?" A pricing model defines how the customer is charged for the offering.[57] Pricing levels determine "price points," or the price charged for a certain level of usage, quantity or service.

Of course generating new revenue streams is a primary reason for innovation. These streams could come from horizontal diversification (acquiring competitors) or vertical diversification (acquiring upstream suppliers or downstream distributors) in your industry. Or it could mean market development and market penetration in your target market segment.

The following are some question that can help guide you in assessing your revenue model:

Financial Model Audit Questions		
1. Which of the revenue models does your organization use? 2. What revenue models are your competitors adopting?	**Question 1**	**Question 2**
o Asset sales		
o Usage fee		
o Flat rate retainer fee		
o Time-based fee		
o Subscription fees		
o Renting/leasing		
o Licensing		
o Brokerage fees		
o Advertising		
o Fixed price		
o Dynamic price		

The following Call to Action provides a brainstorming guide for assessing your current financial model:

Call to Action

Developing a Financial Model

1. Prepare a comparison chart of the price points for your top five competitors.
2. Prepare a function/features comparison chart.
3. Determine if your competitors' value is superior or inferior to yours.

The ability to sustain your financial model is predicated on creating intellectual and human capital in your market development for revenue generation and in your infrastructure for costs efficiencies. There can be differentiation that emerges from developing strong distribution channel relationships and branding such as the "official sponsor" or a certified partner concept. Associating your brand with Microsoft or Cisco could have major revenue implications, especially for smaller firms. Even giants such as General Electric found revenue generating value in developing a joint venture with Hitachi, based on their reputation in the nuclear energy field.

Being part of a partner network or a distribution channel can have significant impact on cost structures. Economies of scale and learning curves are shared with partners to decrease material and logistics costs. Being a part of the supplier network of Walmart can have cost implications. Being part of the Amazon vendor ecosystem can reduce costs while generating access to distribution channels that small firms have not had in the past. Process innovations are shared if you are a valued part of a major companies' supply chain. Sharing CRM databases and user profiles can reduce the costs of customer acquisition and retention.

The Institute for Innovation Revenue Model

Our primary revenue sources come from:

- Software subscriptions and licensing
- Consulting and facilitation fees
- Book sales
- Speaking fees

Our cost efficiencies depend on leveraging technology and a flexible network of Certified Innovation Strategists.

New and Emerging Business Models

There are a number of new and emerging industry level business models which should provide some interesting examples for you to better understand business model innovation. They are also included in the Idea Accelerator database for use in brainstorming. By applying these emerging business models to new opportunities and ideas they can help you innovate your business model.

Airline Industry Business Model Innovations: Airlines are reinventing their industry business model in terms of value proposition, infrastructure, market and financial components. Notice that most only innovate in one basic area of their business model. For example:

- Value proposition: Airlines such as Easy Jet (in Europe), Southwest and Jet Blue have offered value by providing the same service for lower cost. Low-cost airlines have eliminated the major hub system in favor of short-haul direct routes in small markets.
- Key activities: Many airlines are outsourcing reservation systems, catering, travel agencies, retail stores and maintenance. This enables them to focus on narrower parts of the value chain such as: capacity planning, marketing and financial risk management (e.g. oil price hedging).
- Strategic partnership: Airlines have partnered with other airlines to offer through ticketing and shared frequent flyer programs to enhance their network impact and increase customer loyalty.

- Revenue model: Airlines have also enhanced their revenue model by offering credit cards with frequent flyer mileage signing bonuses.
- Cost model: Serving small markets with lower airport fees and operating an older fleet of the same aircraft model lowers operation and maintenance costs for better cost efficiencies.

Telecom Business Model Innovations: A significant new business model that has emerged in the telecommunication mobile market is the mobile virtual network operator (MVNO). An MVNO provides mobile phone services, but unlike traditional carriers does not have its own licensed frequency allocation of radio spectrum, nor does it necessarily have the infrastructure required to provide mobile telephone service. MVNOs have business arrangements with traditional mobile network operators (MNO) to buy minutes of use for resale.

This business model has emerged because of the intersection of two market factors:

- Regulatory intervention designed to lower the barriers for market entry and ultimately increase competition
- A strategic decision by an MNO looking to extend its existing operations and target niche or under-served segments through a second or perhaps multiple brands

The MVNO achieves cost efficiency because it does not spend capital on communication spectrum and infrastructure. From a strategic partnering and distribution channel perspective, there is an advantage for a traditional MNO operating a wholesale MVNO business unit to complement its retail model. Some have engaged potential MVNO partners or have launched their own branded MVNOs.

MVNOs are mostly a European phenomenon operating on the GSM frequency, but they are expecting revenue streams to grow globally. Virgin Mobile UK became the first commercially successful MVNO in 2003. Virgin expanded into the US with Virgin Mobile USA. Sprint Nextel acquired this company in 2009 for nearly USD $483 million.

The telecom industry has also offered other business model innovations based on new product offerings:

- Nextel has developed a technology platform with its walkie-talkie service.
- Direct Connect and Motorola's TETRA have developed public safety networks.
- The UK retailer Car Phone Warehouse offers multi-operator product offerings.
- Sprint PCS developed a multi-level affiliate network build-out model.

Media Industry Business Model Innovations: In the media industry a number of firms have innovated their business model by introducing new value proposition offerings to differentiate themselves from competitors:

- Pixar has created value with its computer generated image (CGI) animation skills and supply-chain configuration models.
- Movie Bank (under the brand name Red Box) has developed a business model around offering an automated self-service DVD rental service.
- News Corp has developed an offering based on content delivery via satellite. It also provides free papers for commuters.

Computer Industry Business Model Innovations: Computer industry business models often focus on value propositions based on differentiating designs, and strategic partnerships for technology and original equipment manufacturers (OEM) such as:

- Apple's design abilities are hard for others to replicate, particularly after being awarded a patent for their multi-touch technology
- Intel has access to chip design and manufacturing technology only marginally differentiated from its competition, but it has excelled at forging partnerships with (OEM) PC manufacturers.
- Microsoft also distinguished itself by becoming embedded in the value chain of OEM.

Functionally-based Business Model Innovation: Some other notable new business models have been based on innovating one or more elements of the business model, such as:

- **Cost.** Walmart is king of the logistics cost model. For example, its trucks always drive with headlights on because data indicates the cost of fewer accidents outweighs the extra fuel consumption. It recycles boxes and pallets while others are throwing them away, and recycles hangers after a purchase.
- **Distribution Channel.** Dell used the Web to develop its distribution channel model. As a result of a build-to-order process, its supply chain infrastructure became lean and more cost efficient in terms of inventory and working capital costs.
- **Customer Relationships.** Gillette maintains branding and customer relationships through the razor handle/blade system and complementary products, like shaving cream and deodorant that have premium margins.
- **Offerings.** Disney's unique branding and characters differentiate it from competitors. Salesforce.com disrupted the industry by charging for software as a service (SaaS model) with a monthly subscription instead of licensing fees.
- **Revenue.** Google became the master of the "pay per click" revenue model by bringing searchers and advertisers together.

Internet based Business Model Innovations: Internet commerce has produced many new kinds of business models. Within the business model framework, it should be considered a special case of infrastructure. Some firms also combine more than one model, such as the blend of software subscription and advertising.

For example, auctions have historically been used to set prices for commodities, fine art, antiquities and financial instruments. eBay used the Internet to revolutionize the auction model by broadening it to apply to a nearly endless list of goods and services. The following is a list of other e-commerce-based business model concepts:

Internet Based Business Model	Example
Brokerage	Orbitz, Priceline, eBay, PayPal, Amazon
Advertising	Yahoo, Monster.com, Craigslist, Google, Nytimes.com
Infomediary	DoubleClick, Nielsen, Edmunds
Community	Red Hat, Wikipedia, Flickr
Merchant	Lands' End, Apple, Amazon, Barnes & Noble
Manufacturer/Direct	Dell
Affiliate	Amazon, Barnes & Noble
Subscription	Netflix, AOL.com, Classmates.com
Utility	Slashdot

Some well-known brands have evolved because of the Internet, but are still challenged in creating a revenue stream. For example, Twitter recently announced a significant change to its business model by introducing advertising on the site. But there may be further challenges. For Twitter's business model there is limited brand loyalty because the Internet creates low barriers of exit for free products and minimal switching costs. Traffic is leveling off due to information overload. Also, it will be difficult to target the market for an advertising strategy to work because it has a broad range of consumers that can't be geographically or demographically segmented.

These emerging business models evolved out of trends in the marketplace. Focus on what prevailing trends could impact your business model—but remember, if everyone sees the trend, you may already be too late. First-mover advantage comes from anticipating disruption. Some of the following Internet business models can help you anticipate potential opportunities and transform them into value:

Other Business Models	Description
Bricks and Clicks	Integrates online and offline presences. Companies may allow customers to order online, but pick up their order at a local store, such as with Walmart's Site-to-Store centers. Lands End allows customer returns at the local Sears.
Disintermediation	The removal of intermediaries in a supply chain such as a distributor, wholesaler, broker, or agent. Companies deal with every customer directly typically at a lower cost of servicing customers directly, such as through the Internet.
Direct sales	A retail channel for the distribution of goods and services. At a basic level, it is marketing and selling products directly to consumers, away from a fixed retail location.
Franchising	Franchising is the practice of using another person's business model. The franchiser grants the independent operator the right to distribute its products, techniques and trademarks for a percentage of gross monthly sales and a royalty fee. Various tangibles and intangibles such as national or international advertising, training and other support services are commonly made available by the franchiser.
Freemium	A business model that offers basic Web services, or a basic downloadable digital product, for free, while charging a premium for advanced or special features. This business model has gained popularity with Web 2.0 companies.

Multi-Level Marketing	Also called network marketing, describes a marketing structure used by some companies as part of their overall marketing strategy. The structure creates a marketing and sales force by compensating promoters of company products not only for sales they personally generate, but also for the sales of other promoters they introduce to the company. This creates a down line of distributors and a hierarchy of multiple levels of compensation in the form of a pyramid.
Professional Open Source	A business model that many open-source software vendors use, in which model partners offer what is perceived as "free" open-source software with paid professional services.
Servitization of Products	Refers to the relative importance of service in a product offering. That is, products today have a higher service component than in previous decades. Virtually every product today has a service component.

Public Sector Operation Models

Business model innovation is applicable to the public sector as well in terms of operation models. The difference is the emphasis on government budget-based revenue instead of market sources in business, and the focus on stakeholder value creation for citizen and constituent rather than on profits and customers.

The public sector is particularly vulnerable to major disruptions caused by the recent economic crisis. The U.S. and many other developed countries are experiencing major budget crises at national and state levels. For the fourth year in a row, most states are facing substantial budget deficits. State budget gaps will total $112 billion for fiscal year 2012, which starts July 1 in most states, according to the Center on Budget and Policy Priorities. Only six states do not project a shortfall. [58]

The cumulative effects of this financial crisis are compounded by the national budget deficit that has reached over $12 trillion. Increasing the federal debt ceiling beyond its current level of $14.3 billion comprises a major threat to the future prosperity in the United States. In 2009, the US ranked 27th globally in terms of the largest deficit as a percentage of GDP. Only Ireland, the United Kingdom, Spain and Greece are Organisation for Economic Co-operation and Development (OECD) countries that have worse deficits than the US. As 2011 closes we have become well aware of the potential for default by many European Union countries and its effect on the global economy.

A number of public sector business or operational models have emerged to transform these disruptions into opportunities and transformational innovation for the benefit of citizens:

- **Internal Transformation**: Features the redesign of service activities currently provided in-house to achieve lasting step-change in performance, cost and customer experience.
- **Outsourcing/Privatization:** Local authorities subcontract key processes, services or whole operations to a third-party organization, while retaining overall ownership and ultimate responsibility.
- **Strategic Partnership:** A formal arrangement between a public body and private sector organization (or consortium) to plan and deliver specific long-term transformation objectives and provide services.
- **Shared Services:** This model has existed as a change option for local government for a number of years. Shared services constitute merging services between organizations and to delivering efficiency savings through reductions to overheads and/or performance improvements.
- **Lead Authority Model**: A public sector organization is led by the parent local authority and establishes best practice solutions with private sector involvement. The lead authority establishes the vehicle and carries out services on behalf of other public (and potentially private) organizations, growing its market share through the provision of a particular range of services.

Outsourcing core government functions is commonly called privatization. Privatization is based on the assumption that commercial businesses can conduct government activities more efficiently on a for-profit basis. Transferring services from the public sector to the commercial and social sectors has become a strategy for reducing deficits without increasing revenue for many government agencies.

I am personally familiar with the privatization of foster care in Florida. My family operated a 50-bed residential and therapy program for adolescent boys ages 8-18 whose parents had their parental rights terminated. In addition to housing, food and clothing, most needed psychological counseling due to experiencing some form of abuse.

In the late 1990s, Florida Governor Jeb Bush's administration encouraged local communities to form tax-exempt organizations to provide foster care related services. Community agencies were motivated to provide better quality care. But the State's interest in cutting costs created funding tensions. As a result of the transition to privatization, profits were erased for businesses that previously averaged 15 percent in net operating profit.

Without the potential for financial reward, the only motivation for personally guaranteeing a working capital line of credit of $100,000 was for "the greater good of society." The uncertainty of revenue sources led to below break even numbers and the eventual closing of facilities. The moral of the story is privatization can be a viable model of outsourcing if the government motivation of cost-cutting can accomplished while retaining fair market profit incentives. However, expecting social entrepreneurs to take on financial risks without the potential for reward, while still subject to bureaucratic uncertainty and inefficiencies, can be unreasonable.

Sustainability in the Public Sector Business Model

The concept of sustaining your business model as intellectual property applies to the public sector as well. Take the case of the consulting firm Accenture. They were awarded a patent in 2005 based on an innovation that was a computer related method for funding a state government procurement system. It comprises the acts of providing a procurement system in an Internet portal for use by a state government agency to communicate electronically to qualified vendor. It provides a payment system and electronic transactions with constituents, an auction inventory and it manages the state government agency reserve fund.

This example demonstrates the importance of using the intellectual property process to make sure your business model is sustainable, regardless of whether it is in the commercial or public sector.

CHAPTER 5

CULTIVATE AN INNOVATION
ECOSYSTEM: KEY #5

"Innovation comes from people meeting up in the hallways or calling each other at 10:30 at night with a new idea, or because they realized something that shoots holes in how we've been thinking about a problem. It's ad hoc meetings of six people called by someone who thinks he has figured out the coolest new thing ever and who wants to know what other people think of his idea…and it comes from saying no to 1,000 things to make sure we don't get on the wrong track or try to do too much." [59]—Steve Jobs

Can Innovation be Systematized?

When Steve Jobs was asked, "How do you systematize innovation?" he responded, "The system is that there is no system." Is this the way to institutionalize innovation? Is it a sustainable approach in a hypercompetitive world to base your hope on the random meeting of six people who eventually come up with a 1-in-1,000 groundbreaking idea?

Such a philosophy may have worked for a genius like Jobs, but let's face it—it's not a reliable method for the rest of us. Consider this ecosystem metaphor: nature is not a random system of organic interactions. Achieving a bountiful harvest requires a systematic approach to planting, irrigating, and cultivating. Human engineering is sometimes required in the ecosystem in addition to the correct blend of moisture, nutrients and radiant energy. All these elements need to be present for consistent conversion of natural resources into fruitful output. In the ecosystem of the organization we need to proactively systematize and institutionalize innovation resources to achieve a future of prosperity.

Since knowledge is the energy source for an innovation ecosystem, the fifth key is to create a systematic way for it to flow from one stakeholder to another so that it adds value at each stage of the process. Waiting for a naturally occurring knowledge ecosystem is neither proactive nor sustainable.

So how does valuable knowledge flow among people in the real world? How can we harness collective intelligence for the good of the organization? You can begin to better understand the process by considering these five mental traits of successful innovative people. Although some of these traits are innate and others result from being part of an inquisitive environment, researchers Dyer and Gregersen suggest these discovery skills can be learned, but they stop short of suggesting how. [60]

1. **Observing**: An ability to closely observe details, particularly people's behavior.
2. **Questioning**: An ability to ask "what if?", "why?", and "why not?" to challenge the status quo and reveal the bigger picture.
3. **Associating**: A cognitive skill that allows creative people to make connections across seemingly unrelated questions, problems or ideas.
4. **Experimenting**: Innovative people are always trying new experiences and exploring new worlds.
5. **Networking**—Creative people are really good at networking with smart people who have little in common with them, but from whom they can learn.[61]

Our Six Step Collective Intelligence system is designed to empower innovation stakeholders. It provides an approach to institutionalize innovation and tools for the development of the skills of the Innovation Strategist in the following ways:

- **Observing:** Assessing the behavior of innovation stakeholders through team building and empowerment exercises.
- **Questioning:** Focusing attention on new challenges and questions.
- **Association:** This is the "special sauce" of our bisociation brainstorming® methodology, where we identify future-focused knowledge from unrelated areas and discover possibilities from the infinite intersections of this knowledge.
- **Experimenting:** Helping innovative ideas evolve by using new and emerging business models.
- **Networking:** Using collaborative technology to bring creative people together with an innovative process and technology.

Six Step Collective Intelligence System

To accelerate and sustain your innovation process you need a system. The Six Step process of the Institute for Innovation harnesses the collective intelligence in your organization. Our proprietary methodology is based on our patent-pending concept called Bisociation Brainstorming®. This methodology is the basis for our strategic innovation consultancy and the Idea Accelerator™, our unique electronic brainstorming software, to be described in Chapter 6.

What are the Six Steps to Collective Intelligence?

1. **Visualize your Strategic Environment**
2. **Explore Future-focused Knowledge**
3. **Discover Future Possibilities**
4. **Innovate New Ideas and Solutions**
5. **Envision Scenarios and Roadmaps**
6. **Measure Effectiveness**

In the next section I will discuss each step and provide a practical tool you can use in your role as the Innovation Strategist to accelerate innovation in your organization and for your clients.

Step 1: Visualize Your Strategic Environment

The first step in stimulating the creative intelligence of your innovation stakeholders is focused attention and focused visualization of your strategic environment. Focused attention is the cognitive process of selectively concentrating on one thing while ignoring other things, and the ability to respond discretely to specific visual, auditory or tactile stimuli. It assists questioning by using the collective intelligence of your stakeholders to achieve consensus on the right questions.

Focused visualization builds on the concept of focused attention. As discussed in the previous chapter, neuroscience research indicates that we can stimulate greater creative brain activity by focusing on new information. Graphic visualization helps the brain focus on new information by creating an organized image and facilitating task consensus in looking at the organization's environment, strategic goals, operational issues, and desired outcome.

Strategic Knowledge Mapping is a graphic visualization technique that focusing on the organization's environment and desired outcomes by creating a mind map. Mind-mapping software creates an image-centered diagram that illustrates semantic or other connections between portions of information, to generate a visual structure that represents key concepts or idea. By presenting these connections in a radial, non--linear graphical manner, it encourages a brainstorming approach and eliminates the hurdle of initially establishing a relevant conceptual framework to work within.

Knowledge mapping presents internal and external knowledge to help make sense of information and stimulate insight. It depicts relationships between knowledge items, groups of people, activities, concepts and terms. Project-based organizations, for instance, will organize information about project teams and best practices. The strategic knowledge map helps organize and focus research and database input.

Figure 5-1 is an example of the visualization stage of a project for the Center for Strategic Studies, on behalf of the Brazilian Ministry of Science and Technology.

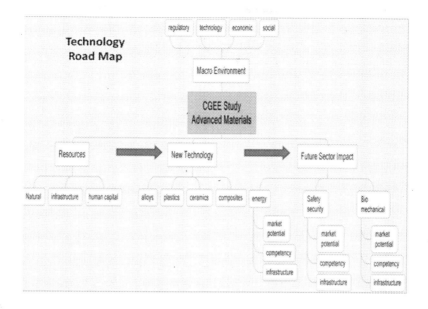

Figure 5-1: The Technology Roadmap provides a template for organizing and focusing research and database input.

In this project the knowledge discovery process began at the macro level by exploring regulatory, technology, economic, and social trends in Brazil's advanced materials sector of the economy. At the industry level, we focused on resources and new technology. The third phase looked at future impact of technology commercialization in the energy, safety, and biomechanical markets.

The outcome of the visualization map was a list of variables, issues and topics that must be researched to discover what new knowledge will impact the future. From this list the project leaders developed a research questionnaire that focused on what was changing at each level of the environment.

Call to Action:

Step 1—Create a Strategic Environment Map

1. Choose from a list of key issues for strategic foresight engagement.
2. Present issues on graphical mind map to ensure a consensus on a comprehensive list.
3. Discuss key variables related to the issues in context of strategic goals and objectives.
4. Review macro environment questionnaire to develop standard research questions.
5. Develop customized research questions.
6. Assign research questions to stakeholders or research team.

Step 2: Explore Future Focused Knowledge

One of the best ways for innovation stakeholders to generate creative solutions is to focus on newly discovered associations. Mednick's associative theory of creative thought--or linking unrelated data to uncover unique insight--supports this concept.[62] Innovation Strategists train their clients or stakeholders to scan the environment for information not only relevant to the future, but from multi-disciplinary fields of data.

Environmental scanning is the process of researching future focused knowledge and sharing strategic information of an organization's macro and industry level environment. Strategic information refers to events or relationships outside the firm that can exploit the firm's strengths, accentuate its weaknesses, or highlight potential threats.

Measuring scanning activity can be difficult because managers scan in fragmented, informal and ad hoc ways. There is a positive link between scanning and the acquisition of strategically relevant, external information with organizational performance. But scanning alone is not enough. The organization's primary strategy can be a contributor to organizational performance and, in fact, may be the source of an organization's distinctive competence.

Technological scanning collects and analyzes external information to make better decisions on technological change and innovation, and to increase the firm's competitiveness. In the corporate planning process there is an assumption that incremental progress in technology will occur. The inherent limitation to an incremental approach is that past developments in a given technology cannot always be extrapolated into the future; every technology has its limits. The key to sustaining a competitive advantage is to anticipate when to shift resources to a technology with more potential.

Unlike other methodologies, our Six Step Collective Intelligence process focuses on researching and extracting dynamic knowledge from diverse domains and multiple levels of the environment. Participants perform environmental scanning prior to the session and bring documented research on dynamic knowledge. This knowledge can relate to information at a variety of global, societal, industrial and organizational levels relevant to the organization.

Macro level environmental knowledge at the global and society level is typically categorized into four groups:

- Economic
- Political-legal-regulatory
- Social-cultural-demographic
- Technological

The secondary level of environmental knowledge is the industry level, which focuses on dynamic knowledge related to a particular industrial sector. At this level, the primary exploration questions are:

- What competitive dynamics are changing the industry?
- Are there disruptive technologies or business models on the horizon?
- Are customer tastes or values changing in terms of function and utility?

As previously mentioned, Porter's Five Forces competitive analysis factors are useful in exploring industry change.

At the micro-level of your strategic environment, research focuses on dynamic knowledge that depicts change for the organization, such as:

- changes in market share
- changes in primary and secondary activities of the value chain
- changes in human capital, production capacity, and support structures

Again, the emphasis is on information concerned with change and its relevance to the future of the industry or organization. The next section describes the concept of **dynamic knowledge** a term I have coined that includes all types of knowledge that depict change in your environment that can be historical, current or expected in the future.

Dynamic Knowledge Scanning: Our unique approach to ideation focuses research and environmental scanning efforts on future-focused information we call dynamic knowledge. Dynamic knowledge is observed or anticipated phenomenon that likely will have an impact on the future. Historically, knowledge has been defined as tacit knowledge, which resides in the minds of individuals, and explicit knowledge, which is articulated, codified, and stored in organizational media. But they depict static information in dormant environments. In reality, knowledge systems are dynamic and complex interactions within an environment, often characterized by vigorous change.

Dynamic knowledge emphasizes foresight rather than hindsight. When expressed in quantitative terms it has the following characteristics:

- Measured observations of change over time, often expressed as an absolute or a percentage of change in value
- Direction of change, often expressed using comparative adjectives such as increase/decrease, higher/lower, more/less
- Magnitude of change expressed as sustained patterns in units of time over which the change occurs.

This changing and chaotic behavior must be viewed from the knowledge system's environmental frame of reference. Dynamic knowledge momentum can be measured in terms of importance of knowledge and in terms of relevance to an industry's competitive environment or an organization's strategic intent. Also, the rate of change is measured in terms of its probability of occurrence in the future. The product of these variables measures the implications of the dynamic knowledge for the future.

Dynamic knowledge can be classified as follows:

- Prevailing trends are sustainable changes in a particular direction--from moderate to long duration--usually based on historical data.
- Emerging issues are recent occurrences that have a probability of continuing in the future that may not have historical data, but have recently materialized as being extremely relevant to the future.
- Expert predictions are an informed opinion that may be based on limited historical data, but has a strong possibility of occurrence in the future.
- Future scenarios are stories about future conditions based on sound information

On a time continuum, patterns of change are indicated in the following diagram:

Figure 5-2: Dynamic Knowledge Continuum

Prevailing Trends

Environmental scanning identifies external factors that can be identified as trends, or changes and events in the environment that might affect an organization.

A trend is expressed as a percent of change, in a direction over a period of time. For example, there has been an "x" percent increase in "y" over "z" time. If the value of change is plotted on a graph, the slope of the curve represents the trend.

Trends can be quantified as a series of historical data that can be projected into the future. For example, forecasting a turning point or a drastic shift of technological change in the economic context can use leading indicators, econometrics, adoption modes and decomposition methods. Some models of environmental scanning forecast the probable environment for change using historical trend data and bridge information gaps by inserting the missing links (interpolation) and extending data points (extrapolation) based on a linear equation. If plotted, the rate of these changes in the organization's environment can be represented by the slope coefficient of the curve.

However, extrapolation models with empirical data have been described as obsolete because major shifts in paradigms and technology are not linear and can't be predicted with historical data. Alternatively, forecasting innovation can be accomplished by integrating conceptually linked measures with expert opinions. Expert opinion can evaluate the significance of linear trend projections qualitatively or quantitatively, in terms of the degree of probability of occurrence and relevance of the phenomenon to the organization's strategic intent.

Consider some examples of trends from an industry report the Institute for Innovation developed for the Research Triangle Regional Partnership (RTRP). Their goal was to develop a five-year strategic plan for the 12-county area around Raleigh-Durham. RTRP engaged 32 "wonks" (policy makers) made up of senior level executives from a cross section of the community, representing private, public and social sectors. Prevailing trends, emerging issues, and expert predictions were researched, shared and evaluated by the group based on the relevance to their goal of economic prosperity and the likelihood of occurring in the future. The subjective ratings using "crowd wisdom" on a 100-point scale resulted in the following top trends:

Dynamic Knowledge Description page 1	category	value
A disturbing trend in law school diversity -- despite steady demand for a more diverse class of law students, improving quality of potential diverse law students, and the rising capacity of diverse law students, law schools have a declining enrollment of almost 10% of African American and Mexican American enrollments.	Education 1	81
Employer demand for workers with "middle skills" (meaning workers with a community college credential) will exceed the available supply by 19,000 positions a year each year between 2007 and 2017. Yet the ability of the community college system to meet the demand is constrained.	Education 2	56
High school graduation rates peaked at 77% in 1969, fell back to 70% in 1990, and have stayed in this range into the current decade. The graduation rate for disadvantaged minorities is thought to be closer to 50%.	Education 3	42
Young, single women are emerging as influential leaders of the "Creative Class" and will make up 60% of college enrollment by 2013. For the first time in US history. Women will comprise the majority of the workforce by 2010.	Education 4	36
World food production must rise by 50 percent by 2030 to meet increasing demand, U.N. chief Ban Ki-moon told world leaders Tuesday at a summit grappling with hunger and civil	Ecology 1	61
State and local governments are increasingly adopting public policies to improve urban quality and to support sustainable economic development and businesses.	Ecology 2	56
Communities are increasingly recognizing that they need to plan to build trusted communications within and among emergency providers, including the media, and must avoid unwarranted belief in any organization's own ability to be resilient in the face of a crisis.	Ecology 3	56

Figure 5-3: Dynamic Knowledge example.

A driver is an energizing force(s) in an organization's external or internal environment that causes the momentum and direction of a trend. Driving forces compete with countervailing forces to accelerate or decelerate the movement of trends. These forces affect the rate, direction and frequency of change. While there are phenwomenon or occurrences in the environment that drive change, they also exhibit the sustained characteristics of trends. For example, the need for convenience is a driving force for a number of trends such as the growth of the fast food industry. But a second order consequence of the proliferation of fast food franchises is the increase in diabetes and obesity. Recent projections suggest that diabetes will affect one of every 30 Americans, and the majority of Americans are considered overweight, as the average weight has increased 20 lbs. in the last 20 years.

This approach to quantifying dynamic knowledge relates well to the concept of the calculus of innovation introduced in Chapter 2. The ranking metric used could correlate to measurements of momentum that are used in physics. In this case, force is the value of the trend in terms of the probability of occurrence (likelihood) and relevance (value). It also can correspond to the value and time matrix used in the innovation life cycle, with value a function of the likelihood of a successful value added activity.

Finally, Step 3 also involves prioritizing this dynamic knowledge using group collaborative evaluation metrics, based on relevance to the organization's strategic goals and the probability of future occurrence. This allows individuals and organizations to focus on the most important and most likely outcomes that are a product of these emerging trends, issues and predictions.

Call to Action

Step 2—Explore Future Focused Knowledge

1. Research trends, emerging issues and expert predictions at the global, society, industry and organization levels.
2. Enter dynamic knowledge into the worksheet template.
3. Upload to Idea Accelerator™ database for sharing and prioritizing.

Step 3: Discover Future Possibilities

What is the "special sauce" in our Six Step Collective Intelligence™ methodology? Step 3 describes our process of discovering infinite possibilities from diverse knowledge by "connecting the dots" from different boxes. At its core, Step 3 is an emergent and exponential ideation process that anticipates disruptions in your environment and possible future outcomes by considering the most likely convergences of dynamic knowledge. To discover the infinite possibilities of opportunities and challenges that can occur, we use a unique blend of associate, lateral, divergent, and convergent thinking methodologies. Unlike other ideation models, this approach optimizes thinking by connecting the dots inside and outside different boxes.

Our process is consistent with Mednick's research on associative thinking that looks for patterns of data from seemingly unrelated areas. It is also similar to lateral thinking, an outside of the box approach popularized by de Bono, which uses a technique called "provocative operations" which looks at a problem from a new perspective. In this technique a proposed idea may not necessarily be the optimum solution, but it does shift thinking patterns away from predictable to unexpected thoughts. The problem is outside of the box thinking can lack reliability when performed outside the boundaries of standard knowledge due to the risk and uncertainty of unsupported theories.

Divergent thinking is the creative generation of multiple answers to a set problem. It draws on ideas from different disciplines and fields of inquiry to reach a deeper level of knowledge, analogous to the concept of "outside of the box thinking." The box is a metaphor for the domain boundaries of conventional knowledge, tacit and explicit.

While divergent thinking generates variability, convergent thinking usually generates orthodoxy by leading to a solution based on existing knowledge rather than knowledge creation. It uses deductive reasoning to generate one optimum answer to a problem, usually where there is a compelling inference. This approach obviously has limited application to innovation since the convergent thinker focuses on a narrowly defined problem and tries to synthesize information and knowledge to achieve a solution.

Bisociation Brainstorming® is the core of our unique creativity methodology for converging dynamic knowledge to discover future possibilities and new ideas. Instead of using divergent thinking that can be chaotic and undisciplined, it takes input from divergent knowledge domains and uses a systematic and repeatable convergent ideation processes. Bisociation is the process of intersecting ideas from two seemingly unrelated things to discover an original thought or idea. Theoretically, the more dissimilar the concepts, the more unexpected and impressive the discoveries can be. Koestler first introduced it in a book called *The Act of Creation*.[63] Koestler suggests bisociation results in greater creativity than using the more familiar and mundane associative (purely logical) thinking. He contrasts bisociation with association, saying that association refers to previously established connections among ideas but bisociation involves making entirely new connections. His work, which addressed creativity in the fields of art, science and humor, led him to conclude that more interesting ideas in the arts come from relating two or more unrelated genres.

Bisociative thinking presumes two independent matrices of perception or reasoning interacting to result in a new fusion, with intellectually challenging effects. These matrices can include any ability, habit, skill or pattern of ordered behavior governed by a code of fixed rules. The more independent the information is, the more unexpected and impressive the achievement—and, subsequently, the more novel the discovery.

In contrast to organizational learning, which is the acquisition of a new knowledge, bisociation is the combination, re-shuffling and re-structuring of new knowledge. The term bisociation is meant to point to the independent, autonomous character of knowledge matrices, which are brought into contact in the creative act, whereas associative thought operates among members of a single pre-existing matrix.

Ko and Butler[64] described bisociative thinking as the missing link between prior knowledge and recognition of entrepreneurial opportunities. They found that bisociation played a significant role in determining whether or not individuals recognized opportunities and why some individuals are capable of entrepreneurial behavior.

Although measured at the individual level, they suggested bisociative thinking ability would be important at all levels of the firm, and nurturing this ability in their employees would result in more novel products.

The concept of bisociation in the creative process holds tremendous promise for explaining the "how" of entrepreneurial innovation from multiple environmental perspectives. A bisociation based visioning process will more often produce that "aha" sensation in the market place if systematically used by your stakeholders.

Examples of Bisociation: The bisociation of prevailing trends has led to a number of new and disruptive business models. Case in point: the increase in people using computers is a technology trend (see Figure 5-3). The increase in people traveling is a social trend. Using bisociation to converge these trends reveals a new business model: Internet travel booking. This has created a giant market during the past decade that would not have evolved by following only one of the two trends. In fact, Orbitz and Expedia, two online booking sites, were sold for a combined market value of over $6 billion.

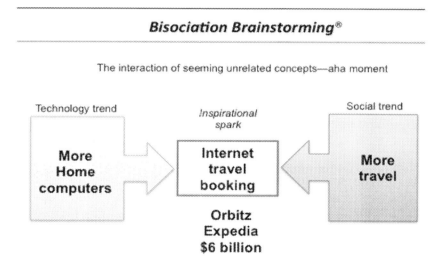

Figure 5-4: A convergence of two trends resulted in an entirely new business model.

Exciting new business models are evolving from the convergence of two or more existing concepts. Zynga, a San Francisco-based social gaming company, capitalized on the convergence of video gaming and social media to create a new market called social gaming, which is taking video gaming viral (see Figure 5-5). Instead of playing with the computer or the person on the couch next to you, you can create and interact with a community of fellow players. This market was made possible because Facebook went from one million users in 2004 to 600 million in 2010.[65] Zynga grossed $850 million in 2010.

Figure 5-5: The convergence of two trends led to a new business model called social gaming.

In fact their 47 percent profit margin when compared to Google's 29 percent and Apple's at 28 percent was touted as the most profitable ever by Business Insider. [66] This is after Zynga pays royalties in the form of advertising to acquire users and 30 percent of virtual goods sales to Facebook. Of course their virtual goods product offering does not cost much to produce, nothing to store as inventory, and does not need a sales force.

Another example is a start-up company called iFly developed an air taxi service for providing short trips between local airports for corporate executives. This opportunity came from the convergence of two trends: There was the technological development of a four-person micro jet with fuel efficient engines and the additional hurdles to traveling posed by political and regulatory issues associated with 911 security procedures.

Bisociation Brainstorming® converges dynamic knowledge in order to discover future possible outcomes, i.e. opportunities or challenges based on the possible permutations of combinations for each set of dynamic knowledge, taken two or more at a time. Because these permutations can be potentially voluminous, the Idea Accelerator™ software algorithms help prioritize possibilities based on the average score of converged dynamic knowledge.

Accelerating Opportunity Recognition

Our Collective Intelligence model relates opportunity recognition to pattern recognition—the process through which individuals perceive emergent patterns among diverse and seemingly unrelated stimuli or events. Because of their unique knowledge structures and mind sets, some people perceive patterns among emerging changes in technology, markets, demographics, etc., that others overlook.

Ko and Butler concluded that people proficient at opportunity recognition have better developed prototypes of business opportunities. They also use a richer set of mental constructs during ideation than other people and may possess highly efficient working memories. Their model suggests training individuals in effective search strategies can make them more effective at recognizing opportunities.

Stimulating organizational knowledge and learning to create a culture of innovative ideas and collaborative efforts is critical. Collective creativity occurs when two or more people share bisociation. This collaborative creativity is manifested in brainstorming sessions performed with key managers and stakeholders.

Similar to the high energy produced by a particle accelerator in physics, focused attention on the infinite possible interactions of dynamic knowledge produces high energy insights. If these waves of energy are directed in a systematic rather than random manner, orderly interference will produce more opportunities for insight and foresight.

Based on cognitive psychology theories, this divergent knowledge and convergence process stimulates new neuron pathways in the brain by systematically focusing on the infinite permutations of dynamic knowledge, thereby increasing the likelihood of insightful discovery. In this knowledge system, the output from the interaction of these "waves" of knowledge results in a unique ability to anticipate possible future disruptions, which can come in the form of opportunities and challenges.

Opportunities are favorable future outcomes for the industry or organization. They manifest themselves as positive situations in which gains are likely and over which the organization has limited control. Challenges are unfavorable future outcomes, or negative situations in which losses are likely and over which one has relatively little control.

In general, strategists primarily focus environmental scanning efforts on searching for opportunities, whereas threats are of secondary interest. More specifically, firms engaged in proactive strategy implementation look for opportunities, whereas reactive managers will scan for challenges. Of course, a natural tendency for growth-oriented firms and new ventures is to focus on opportunities in the entrepreneurial planning process.

To overcome the brain's natural resistance to change, repeated attention must be given to interconnecting new neuron paths. This process enhances mental capabilities, rewires the brain for insight, and allows for "outside the box thinking." Based on these cognitive psychology theories, the 6 Step Collective Intelligence™ methodology stimulates synapses in the brain by systematically focusing on the infinite permutations of dynamic knowledge, thereby increasing the likelihood of insightful discovery.

This interactive approach stimulates a higher order brainstorming process that can be systematized, replicated and institutionalized. When anticipating the next big idea, more surprising predictions for the future can be realized by looking at interactive events and the divergence and convergence of technologies with other phenomena in the environment.

The beauty of this collective intelligence approach is that it allows Innovation Strategists to systematically rethink the future and anticipate future possibilities with consistency. An example from one of our Brazilian projects related to medical heart stints. The researchers on the project indicated that Brazil, on a scale of 1 to 10, was a 5 while the U.S. science was an 8. Our recommendation was not to try to plan how to catch up to the U.S. The question was redirected to determine what is the predicted science that will lead to 10?

Sports analogies work well for illustrating this concept. Sometimes I invoke professional hockey legend Wayne Gretsky. When he was asked the secret of his success, he said, "Because I skate to where the puck is going to be, not to where the puck is." In Brazil I changed the analogy to

Pele anticipating the passing lane in *futbol*, and the point was made. (Of course, I changed the analogy to Michael Jordan anticipating the passing lanes when I working on projects in North Carolina). The most important lesson in this example provided direction on how to target the research of the Brazilian scientists on future-focused dynamic knowledge, rather than the usual data from dated scientific reports.

So how *do* you determine what the science or technology of 10 is going to be? You cannot glean it from academic journals. As an academic, I am very aware that the normal cycle of publishing research is at least three to five years. By the time you design the study, get funding, conduct the study, write the results, get peer reviewed through at least a two cycles of revisions and get it accepted and published, the "puck" is no longer where it used to be.

You must direct your researchers to find out where the "puck" is going to be, skate to that point and wait for its arrival. How does this translate into strategic foresight? One way is finding out what research is being funded in the future.

A good indicator in the United States is what request for proposals are being initiated by the National Science Foundation, the National Institute for Health, the Defense Advanced Research Planning Agency (DARPA), Small Business Innovation Research Grants and the Small Technology Transfer Research grant programs. By scouring these sources you will find out what the top needs are in the government, and what the top scientists think are the most important research priorities. Many of these projects have high expectations that the technology applications will have significant commercialization potential.

So what is anticipating the future worth to you and your organization? Are you satisfied with uninspiring ideas or are you willing to invest the extra time and energy to realize true insight? More importantly, can you translate this insight into meaningful ideas? The next step is designed to translate opportunity into value.

The pyramid in Figure 5-6 provides a very simple graphic visualization template to facilitate steps 3, 4 and 5 in the Idea Accelerator™ process. This

PDF formatted template can be accessed with free Adobe Reader software. After completion, the form can be e-mailed into a cloud application that can then be uploaded into the database.

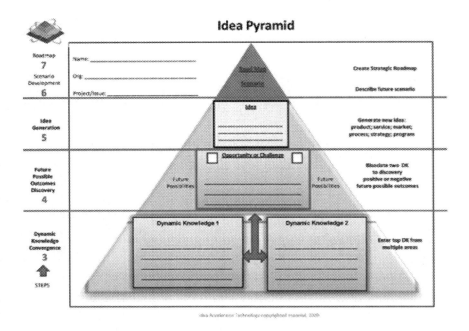

Figure 5-6. The Idea Pyramid is a graphic template for focusing attention on steps 3 through 5 that can be uploaded to the Idea Accelerator™ database.

Call to Action
1. Using the Idea Pyramid (figure 5-6), enter two brief descriptions of dynamic knowledge data.
2. Bisociate the two dynamic knowledge variables to discover future possible outcomes (FPOs).
3. Categorize FPO's in terms of positive or negative future outcomes.

Step 4: Innovate New Ideas and Solutions

In this step of our Six Step Collective Intelligence methodology you will innovate with new ideas by recognizing opportunities that resolve, take advantage of, or mitigate future possibilities that result from convergence of future trends. As an Innovation Strategist you can use this innovation system for think tanks and national and international planning agencies that focus on "big picture" or macro issues such as poverty, the availability of clean water, security, health epidemics and global competitiveness. This system can be applied to regional development agencies that focus on education, talent recruitment, infrastructure, economic competitiveness, and health care. Organizations can also use this collective intelligence system to develop strategic plans that identify their long-term goals and objectives to achieve their vision and missions.

For each of these perspectives, the key is to focus on new ideas that can create value from opportunities recognized at every level. This can include new business models, products, technologies and strategies.

New ideas evolve from systematic and focused attention on the most relevant and probable opportunities and challenges discovered in previous steps. The ideation evolution process is based on the concept that the best ideas are iterative, with each version an improvement of the previous until the final solution is optimized.

Prioritized and appended contributions from other group members that improve the solution are shared online using brainstorming and brainwriting techniques. New ideas are scored and ranked based on potential value and probability of success. Using a collaborative metric, the high-valued ideas are identified, refined and shared.

Solution Evolution

History indicates that great ideas are not a one-time discovery, but rather the "social evolution" of ideas from different sources or inventors. In his book, *The Group Genius*, Keith Sawyer[67] discusses inventions such as the airplane. The primary intellectual capital for its design did not come from the work of the Wright Brothers. The design evolved by subsequent engineering ideas that ultimately led to a more efficient design. Similarly, we encourage participants to append, clarify or amplify the ideas of others rather than compete with or minimize them. Rather than criticizing others' ideas so yours seem better, our system encourages participants to build on existing ideas.

Using the list of emerging business models provided in Chapter 4 can enhance solution evolution. Bisociating an idea with an existing business model, particularly an Internet-based model will stimulate a more informed solution or value proposition.

Call to Action

Step 4—Innovate a New Idea or Solution

1. Using the Idea Pyramid, innovate a new idea: a product, service, market, program, policy or strategy that takes advantage of an opportunity or mitigates a challenge previously identified.
2. Upload the new idea to the database for evaluation and prioritization.
3. Using Idea Accelerator™ software, consider the evolution of a solution to improve clarity or value.
4. Take each idea and try to improve on it by applying a known or emerging business model from Chapter 5.
5. Try to provide more clarity by restating the value proposition.

Step 5—Envision Scenarios and Roadmaps

Scenarios: These stories about an alternate future are a useful tool for understanding the dynamics of change, and providing frameworks for structuring descriptions of alternate and plausible futures. They are decision-focused views of the future based on the insight and perceptions of stakeholders.

Most scenario development techniques are based on the model originated by Shell Oil Company. It starts with the assumption that you have considered all of the many possible futures and you have selected the four best ideas. Our methodology, if used before this stage, improves the likelihood that the scenario you develop has been vetted with a systematic and iterative process of considering many trend interactions to discover possible future possible outcomes.

By considering many future possibilities you can, with greater confidence, tell a story of what happens in the future if one of these ideas—a new product, market, technology or policy—is implemented. In other words, how does the future look for the society, industry or the organization because of the proposed change? Participants develop scenarios for each prioritized idea that describes, in narrative format, the future impact of the new idea on the general society and relevant industries. We can then examine the trajectory or second-order consequences of a number of scenarios.

Scenario development techniques include creating a newspaper headline from the future or writing a movie script based on the new invention or innovation. Using the Idea Accelerator™ methodology, participants analyze the potential impact of each idea at the organizational, departmental or functional level. At each stage participants evaluate future impact and relevance to the industry. The dynamic knowledge database is prioritized based on the group average scores of the two variables. From these scenarios strategies can be developed for contingency planning, risk assessment, and as a basis for continuous monitoring of the environment.[68]

Road Maps: Strategic and technology road maps are a graphic depiction of an action plan that incorporates the development of successful prototyping of new ideas generated. These maps identify the technological, resource and infrastructure requirements, as well as a timeframe necessary for a successful implementation of an action plan. The road map process identifies the following gaps in the implementation of the strategic or technology plan:

- Technological performance
- Human resources
- Financial investment
- Market potential
- Infrastructure

Call to Action

Step 6—Envision Scenarios and Roadmap

1. Write a headline for a newspaper that depicts life in 2020 based on the implementation of your idea.
2. Write a short play or movie script for a day in the life video of a family benefiting from your innovative idea.

Step 6: Measure Effectiveness

Truly actualized innovation must be measurable and often it is an elusive goal. Historically, innovation at the national and organizational level has been measured in terms of patents filed and/or approved. At the organizational level, innovation has been measured in terms of R&D expenditures as a percentage of firm revenue. The first metric rewards scientific discovery; the second rewards research effort, but not results. Neither metric rewards the commercialization and conversion of intellectual property into economic revenue or social value. Some organizations measure innovation based on the number of new products that are in the corporate portfolio over a time horizon of five years or more -- a long window of time to measure efforts.

Step 6 measures the effectiveness of innovation using a modified version of the **Balanced Scorecard**. It is perfectly aligned with the four basic components of the Business Model. It comprises the four following perspectives:

1. **Financial Perspective:** Assesses improvements in cost structure and increased asset utilization that improves productivity. The goal is to identify the metrics that measure the successful development of new revenue sources and increased revenue volume that result from the business model innovation. These metrics would measure enhanced customer value and revenue opportunities that determine growth. This Balanced Scorecard dimension relates to the Financial Model of the Business Model. Some of these metrics would include:

Revenue:

- Sales growth
- Growth in the number of new accounts or customers
- Market share growth

From the cost perspective the productivity strategy set metric parameters for better asset utilization and reduced costs in the internal and external aspects of the value network.

Costs:

- Operating profit margins
- Net profit margins
- Asset turnover
- Inventory turnover
- Return on assets
- Return on equity
- Times interest earned

2. **Customer Perspective:** Measures product/service attributes that improve the customer value proposition. These metrics relate to the Target Market part of the Business Model. Some of these metrics would include:

- Price sensitivity analysis
- Customer satisfaction
- Brand recognition
- Customer retention rates
- Features/functionality
- Distribution channel availability

3. **Internal Perspective:** These metrics measure operations management processes; customer management processes; innovative processes; and regulatory and social processes. This Balanced Scorecard dimension relates to the Infrastructure part of the Business Model. Some of these metrics would include:

- Production efficiency of products and services (reject rates, reprocessing costs
- Distribution of products or services (deliver time)
- Customer value (returns, reviews)
- Percentage of revenue generated by new products
- Number of law suits or fines, employee community service hours

4. **Learning and Growth:** Includes innovations in human, informational and organizational capital (Value Proposition), as measured by patent filings and research publications.

The **Innovation Balanced Scorecard Roadmap** shown in Figure 5-7 demonstrates the inter-relationships among these core perspectives. This template is available at the resource link provided in the electronic version of the book.

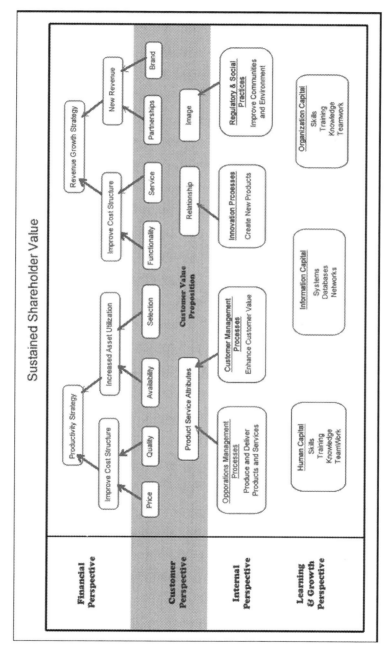

Figure 5-7. The Innovation Balanced Scorecard provides numerous data points and references for measuring the effectiveness of innovation.

171

Call to Action

Measure Effectiveness

1. Identify metrics and key success factors for Financial Model
   a. Productivity costs
   b. Asset utilization
   c. Revenue growth
2. Identify metrics and key success factors for Customer Perspective
   a. Price strategy
   b. Quantity
   c. Availability
   d. Model selection
   e. Functionality
   f. Service
   g. Partnerships
   h. Brand
3. Identify metrics and key success factors for Internal Perspective
   a. Production
   b. Customer management
   c. New products
   d. Community and environment
4. Identify metrics and key success factors for Learning and Growth Perspective
   a. Human capital
   b. Information capital
   c. Organization capital

Institutionalizing Innovation for Success

This chapter covered the essence of the Institute for Innovation's six step process for harnessing the creative intelligence in your organization. Once you, as an Innovation Strategist have mastered these concepts, you'll be ready to facilitate the process by employing our Idea Accelerator™ software, described in the next chapter.

CHAPTER 6

ENGAGE WITH COLLABORATIVE
TECHNOLOGY: KEY #6

"None of us is as smart as all of us."—Japanese Proverb

Innovation 2.0 Technology

Great things can happen when collaboration, assisted by technology, allows the best and most innovative ideas to come forward not just from outside a company, but from throughout the world. Just as organisms in a natural environment are co-dependent for sustenance and growth, innovation stakeholders rely on the collective intelligence of their peers to enhance the pool of existing knowledge. The sixth key is that Collective intelligence goes into hyper-drive when it is fueled by **Innovation 2.0 Technology.**

An ecosystem approach to brainstorming must allow companies and organizations to harness their creative energies by breaking down artificial boundaries that limit knowledge transfer (energy) between stakeholders. It must be flexible enough to incorporate the effective elements of traditional brainstorming sessions. Additionally, it must have the structure and discipline to synthesize multidimensional elements in a dynamic environment to achieve true "outside the box" thinking. These are the characteristics of organic learning that are present in an innovation ecosystem that enables stakeholders to share knowledge in a dynamic and interdependent environment.

This ecosystem approach should also contain the elasticity to be as simple or as complex as the project requires. It must be circular enough to allow a systematic and interactive approach to finding the final actionable idea. This means that the "big idea" from one session can become the subject of innovation in another session, further refining the discovery in each iterative cycle of collaboration. It must provide a way to report each element of knowledge that contributed to the final idea/innovation selected for action or development.

The Limitations of Traditional Brainstorming

Traditional brainstorming sessions, where bright people gather in a room and throw thoughts and ideas around, have been the business world's traditional approach to collaborative innovation, as demonstrated by Apple. Our collaborative technology will enable the Innovation Strategist to address these challenges and provide solutions to these limitations as indicated in the following chart.

Challenges		Solutions
Limited time for strategic planning and brainstorming	**Time**	Perpetual planning and brainstorming.
Costly face to face meetings for geographically dispersed teams	**Distance**	Remote global web-based collaboration
Output from previous strategic planning session is lost	**Continuity**	Electronic archive of planning output
Intellectual capital is in the minds of managers and stakeholders	**Access**	Universal access to intellectual capital
Silos of knowledge and organizational boundaries impede collaboration	**Teamwork**	Facilitated collaboration with internal and external stakeholders

Figure 6-1: Factors that inhibit the efficiency of group creativity include time, distance, continuity, access and teamwork.

Collaborative technology provides unique tools that enable ongoing brainstorming. It addresses the time limitation for strategic planning and brainstorming by enabling it to be perpetual. It reduces the cost of global collaboration with remote web-based collaboration. Innovation 2.0 enables global access to electronic outputs of intellectual capital by internal and external stakeholders. Finally it overcomes group barriers by enabling teamwork in learning networks with diverse perspectives. Innovation 2.0 is the state of the art in terms of group decision support for Collaborative Innovation Networks.

Collaborative Innovation Networks

A collaborative innovation network (CIN) draws on collective intelligence. It is a "cyber team" of self-motivated people with a collective vision, enabled by the Web to collaborate in achieving a common goal by sharing ideas, information and work,"[69] according to Peter Gloor, a research scientist at MIT Sloan's Center for Collective Intelligence and originator of the term. CINs use Internet-based tools for information sharing, thereby enhancing creativity, collaboration and communication.

In the ecosystem vein, Dr. Norman Johnson created the Symbiotic Intelligence Project[70], which focuses on how people create new knowledge by accessing and using information on networks. It assumes that creating an ecosystem based on the symbiotic combination of humans and smart networks will result in collective problem identification and solutions previously undiscovered. Similar to the ecosystem concept of co-evolution symbiotic intelligence supports the premise of this chapter—that collaborative technology can improve the social context of the ideation process.

Several concepts of CIN have evolved recently, including open innovation and crowdsourcing.

Open Innovation: Open innovation is a paradigm that assumes firms can and should use external ideas as well as internal ideas, and internal and external paths to market, as the firm looks to advance their technology. As previously illustrated in our ecosystem metaphor, open innovation demonstrates permeable boundaries between a firm and its environment in which innovations can easily transfer between internal and external stakeholders. In a global economy it has become more difficult for organizations to rely entirely on their own knowledge and research. More companies like Google are growing through acquiring patents or licensing processes from other companies. Others are taking advantage of unused intellectual property through licensing, joint ventures and spin-offs. [71]

Some examples of open innovation include the following:

- **NineSigma** was the first open innovation services provider helping client companies develop and maximize value from their innovation programs. Dr. Mehran Mehregany, of Case Western University, started NineSigma in 2000. In 2008, NineSigma was one of the fastest growing private companies in the U.S. and ranked among the top 20 percent of companies on the Inc. 5000 list.
- **InnoCentive** sources R&D for biomedical and pharmaceutical companies by providing connection and relationship management services between "seekers" and "solvers." Seekers are companies searching for solutions to critical challenges. Solvers are the 185,000 registered members of the InnoCentive crowd that volunteer their solutions to the seekers. Solvers, whose solutions are selected by the seekers, are compensated for their ideas by InnoCentive, which acts as broker.
- **Innovation Exchange** focuses on business problems related to product, service, process and business model innovation. Companies sponsor challenges that are responded to by individuals, or people working in ad hoc teams.
- **Bright Idea** provides social innovation management software to power open innovation communities and contests.
- **Spigit** provides a platform that can create open communities to capture, evaluate, contribute to and select ideas for implementation. Among those using Spigit are private organizations or businesses extending idea communities to customers or partners, or government agencies creating open communities to capture ideas from citizens.
- **PRESANS** is a startup out of the Ecole Polytechnique in France to develop and implement a multi-step dynamic expert sourcing

(MDES) approach, which relies on state-of-the-art, web-mining technology and a multi-step problem-solving process.

Crowdsourcing is a distributed problem solving and production model in which problems are broadcast as an open call for solutions to an unknown group of solvers. "The crowd" forms online communities and submits solutions. The online crowd sorts through the solutions, finding the best solutions, which are owned by the entity that broadcast the problem, while the winning individuals receive a reward.

Using crowdsourcing to solve problems can be explored at comparatively little cost, and often very quickly. Participating organizations pay based on results that come from tapping into a wider range of talent than exists among their current stakeholders. By listening to the crowd, organizations gain first-hand insight into their customers' desires.

An interesting example of a disruptive business model that grew out of Crowdsourcing is iStockphoto, which started as a free image-sharing exchange used by a group of graphic designers. It created a marketplace for the work of amateur photographers who charge between $1 and $5 for a basic image that can be downloaded on the Internet. Industry leaders at first fought iStockphoto and other microstock agencies like ShutterStock and Dreamstime. Eventually, however, Getty Images, the largest traditional agency purchased iStockphoto in 2006 for $50 million.

There has been a recent example of using crowdsourcing to conduct brain research. More than 100 centers and 200 scientists worldwide have collaborated on a database of brain scans for over 21,000 people[72].

Crowdfunding is a similar business model that has the potential to disrupt the current approach to venture funding. The current model of venture funding involves presenting business plans to investors such as angel investors and venture capitalist that require significant returns on investment. Very few start up companies get funding this way. After the financial crisis banks are more unwilling to finance start-ups or even established entrepreneurs.

In 2012 the U.S. Congress passed the CROWDFUND Act (Capital Raising Online While Deterring Fraud and Unethical Non-Disclosure) as part of the JOBS Act (Jumpstart Our Business Startups Act) which will:

- Allow entrepreneurs to raise up to $1 million per year through an SEC-registered crowdfunding portal.
- Free people to invest a percentage of their income. For investors with an income of less than $100,000, investments will be capped at the greater of $2,000 or 5% of income. For investors within an income of more than $100,000, investments will be capped at 10% up to $100,000.
- Require crowdfunding portals to provide investor protection, including investor education materials on the risks associated with small issuers and illiquidity.[73]

Senate amendments include the following provisions:

- Crowdfunding platforms will be required to register with the SEC and an income-based cap will be created to limit the amount that unaccredited investors can contribute.
- Companies participating in crowdfunding will still have to file information with the SEC including the names of officers, major investors, and financial information. Those raising under $100,000 will be required to provide tax returns and financial statements certified by a principle of the company.
- Companies seeking to raise up to $500,000 must file financial statements that have been reviewed by a certified public accountant. And those raising more than $500,000 will have to provide fully audited financial statements.[74]

In this emerging model crowdfunding sites can provide a platform for nascent entrepreneurial ventures to access investment capital from every day people in exchange for shares, products, services or cash. This model of fundraising for new ventures is particularly interesting for countries that do not have an established institutional investment infrastructure, which is the case in most of the emerging global markets.

Group Support Systems

Group support systems (GSS) are computer-based systems that support groups of people engaged in a common task and provide an interface to a shared environment. These systems are designed to help groups become more productive by supporting the exchange of ideas, opinions and preferences and have dramatically increased group productivity.

They are able to do the following:

- Increase quality involvement by providing feedback, while decreasing the corresponding time and effort required for the process
- Foster collaboration, communication and negotiation among group participants
- Combine communication, computing and decision support technologies to facilitate formulation and solution of unstructured problems in a group setting
- Generate a greater quantity of ideas, although after considering redundancy, not necessarily more unique ideas

GSS have evolved beyond the original orientation toward decision making to include electronic meeting systems (EMS), computer-supported collaborative work (CSCW), and groupware, such as electronic brainstorming systems (EBS).

Electronic Brainstorming Systems

Electronic brainstorming systems (EBS) use computers to allow members to interact and to exchange ideas, define the scope of a problem, identify possible solutions, and develop a heuristic classification scheme. By allowing parallelism, stakeholders are able to work in multiple groups on multiple projects simultaneously. Providing a platform that can be anonymous means results can be based on merit, rather than rank in the organizational structure or political maneuverings.

Innovative organizations need an EBS environment to review, organize, consolidate and understand ideas, evaluate their merits, converge on similar ideas, eliminate irrelevant ideas, and obtain participant consensus expeditiously. Because brainstorming encourages creative, diverse and uncensored ideas, many comments are unrefined. The frustration and time spent refining them may cause user satisfaction and productivity to decline and unique ideas lost. Convergent tasks such as idea organization create problems of equivocality during synthesis; consolidation and consensus building cannot be resolved by passive groupware design. Consequently, there is a need for a more proactive and intelligent groupware solution. Our Idea Accelerator™ software is an EBS that provides a collaborative innovation in an Enterprise 2.0 environment and resolves some of the limitations of previous EBS offerings.

Idea Accelerator™ Software

The Idea Accelerator™ software is a proprietary EBS based on research conducted by the Institute for Innovation. We call it Innovation 2.0 because it incorporates Web 2.0 features, such as wikis, blogs, web crawling and discussion forums. It provides a crowdsourcing platform and decision theatre for multiple users to synchronously discover, evaluate and share new knowledge and ideas. The software is designed to provide an enterprise platform for stakeholders to collaborate in the collective intelligence development methodology provided in Chapter 5. The details of the features and functions of the software as they relate to the Six Step Collective Intelligence™ methodology are provided in a companion workbook.

Idea Accelerator™ software enables creativity by focusing attention on the convergence of strategic knowledge and encouraging participants to process new information. Participants can come up with new ideas that take advantage of opportunities (or mitigate challenges). Ideation evolution is based on the concept that the best ideas are iterative, with each version an improvement of the previous, until the final solution is optimized. Ideas are prioritized, and appended contributions are shared online using brainstorming and brainwriting techniques. The online version of the ideation pyramid provides an additional step, called *solution evolution,* where ideas (1.0) can be incrementally appended (1.1) and radically improved (2.0).

Participants based on success probability and potential value product score new ideas. This "new idea map" is plotted using these two scoring factors. Participants can select new ideas to create scenarios that illustrate the future impact of the new idea at two customizable levels, e.g. society or industry, and organization or department.

Written scenarios create a narrative of how the implemented idea will change the environment in the long term. Participants can develop scenarios for each prioritized idea that describes, in narrative format, the future impact of the new idea on the general society and any relevant industries. Participants analyze the potential impact of each idea at the organizational, departmental or functional levels. At each stage participants collaborate and evaluate the future impact and relevance to industry.

To stimulate discussion and further enlightenment, scenarios can be developed to describe the future impact of the implementation of a new idea in narrative form. The chart in Figure 6-2 is the export from the scenarios developed by the Research Triangle Regional Partnership project. This narrative can address future implications at customizable levels, including society, industry, organization, function, department, task or person.

EI-210	Global warming destroys 40% of housing on North Coast due to rising Sea levels
EI-203	Hayes finally becomes President of Region—eliminating all governmental jurisdiction
EI-211	INC system wins national award as the most effective economic development support University of all 50 states.
EI-204	N.C. State University's Centennial Campus celebrates 50th anniversary. Governor James B. Hunt Jnr. (serving 8th term) declares experiment an unbridled success. Jobs created and capital investment at centennial exceed vaunted Research Triangle Park
EI-206	NC population boom/growth has been kept in check, with energy needs—"Nuclear energy was the correct Choice"
EI-208	Quintiles completes closure of RTP office—transition to New Hanover complete.

EI-212	Rural—50% of working population generates income from home—"telecommuting"
EI-205	Rural Areas become the most popular place to live and work as over-population forces people from Raleigh/Durham
EI-209	Space travel becomes a little more affordable for citizens.
EI-207	Triangle Universities together have cracked the genetic code of cancer that will lead to a cure.

Figure 6-2: Coming up with different scenarios is part of the impact analysis.

The other stage of envisioning is the graphic development of *strategic and technology road maps.* These illustrate the milestones, gaps and steps necessary to achieve the new idea articulated in the narrated scenario. They are a graphic visualization of requirements necessary for implementation including: capital, infrastructure, human resources, collaborative partnerships and scientific innovation.

The Idea Accelerator™ provides reports that detail each of the emergent steps in the process attributable to the new ideas or courses of action identified. The report gives the dynamic knowledge, related scores, comments, and documentation, opportunities and/or challenges associated with the idea, associated scenarios, scoring, and comments. It can be exported to a spreadsheet as part of the deliverables of the strategic innovation project.

Virtual Collaboration

The inter-group sharing of the collective intelligence of internal and external stakeholders improves the quality of collaboration. Database administrators can provide read-only or evaluation privileges as appropriate. Group facilitators can initiate discussions on each idea via the Microsoft SharePoint Portal discussion forum to elaborate on potential disruptions, opportunities, challenges and new ideas generated by their group or other groups in the organizational ecosystem.

Idea Accelerator™ eliminates the traditional constraints of collaboration. It facilitates teamwork for diverse, geographically dispersed external and internal stakeholders. Also, it provides a tool for perpetually planning, with remote web access as well as an electronic archive that allows universal stakeholder access to the organization's intellectual capital. These features provide a terrific tool for providing a network of innovation stakeholders with an innovation system that is systematized and institutionalized.

CHAPTER 7

MAKE INNOVATION VIRAL: KEY #7

"We wanted to build a new communications medium.
We knew we'd be successful when we were no longer cool
-- when we were such an integral part of people's lives that
they took us for granted."—Mark Zuckerberg, founder of
Facebook

Contagious Innovation

When it comes to spreading viruses, as with a biological disease or
computer dysfunction, it can spell disaster. But when innovation becomes
a viral, self- replicating process, contagiousness, a term coined by Malcolm
Gladwell in his best-selling book, *The Tipping Point*,[75] becomes a critical
ingredient for success. In other words, the seventh key is to ensure that
innovation is not an isolated event but an infectious epidemic of positive
change.

While a viral campaign can be delivered by word of mouth, today it
can spread exponentially faster via the Internet. Viral campaigns require
the networking skills of a thought leader in networking and enabling
technology. The enabling technology will "make it sticky," using the
vernacular of Gladwell.

Facebook is a good example of innovation going viral. What started out as
a dorm room prank to get guys to rate pictures of Harvard girls went viral
overnight and crashed the University computer server. Using the basic
concept of human attraction based on physical appearance was a visceral

trigger, fueling a social networking revolution that is still experiencing exponential viral growth.

The Innovation Strategist as a Thought Leader

The term thought leader typically is used to describe a person who is widely recognized among peers for innovative ideas and cutting-edge expertise in a given field, with the ability to promote those ideas to a large audience.

Thought leaders are systems thinkers who take an organic, scientific approach to their respective disciplines. As system thinkers they analyze their discipline from a holistic perspective.

Thought leaders present insightful, provocative and compelling perspectives that frame the way people think about key issues and guide them to smarter decisions. They encourage people to rewire their brains with new information and produce unique outcomes. If they can get people to think and act differently, they enable innovation; otherwise they are just sharing information.

Gladwell describes agents of social epidemics as connectors, mavens and salesmen. Connectors know many people from several different social realms; when they get close to an idea, the idea becomes more powerful. Mavens not only collect information, they share it, becoming social and information experts. But, typically, mavens are not persuaders. Salesmen are those people who encourage others to try a new idea and make it almost impossible to resist.

Innovation Strategists exhibit the characteristics of a thought leader. They have a network with which they share information and convince their stakeholders of the value of their ideas. Innovation Strategists must make ideas "stickier" if they are to stay with their networks long enough to produce results. They often facilitate the diffusion of innovation through stages. First, as innovators they are early adopters. In subsequent stages of diffusion-- early majority, late majority and last movers, and laggards-- they fill in the gaps that move the idea from an embryonic seed to a fully developed and harvested fruitful idea that is commercialized for added value.

Engaging the Crowd through Social Networks

Social media platforms such as LinkedIn and Facebook can provide powerful vehicles for developing an Innovation Strategist's social network. Comments in discussion groups and the responses of other thought leaders in a discussion thread can determine the relevance and impact of an Innovation Strategist.

The social network potential of thought leaders also can be achieved by engaging in the following activities:

- group memberships
- leadership roles
- publication, editing, and contributing to non-electronic media
- publication, editing, and contributing to electronic media (websites, blogs)
- frequency of past distribution of information within their network.

Thought leaders are most effective when they can make innovation viral. In viral marketing these thought leaders are called alpha users because of their communications, connectivity with core members of their stakeholder community, and their influence over other thought leaders. [76] They often achieve this connectivity using social networks such as Facebook, LinkedIn and Twitter. A social network is a social structure made up of individuals (or organizations) called "nodes," which are interdependent.

Thought leaders create social relationships between stakeholders to generate social capital. Social capital is the value individuals get from being in a social network. They can be influential in spreading either positive or negative information about an innovation, particularly during the evaluation stage of the innovation-decision process and late adopters.

Thought leaders can also act as opinion leaders within a social system. Opinion leaders typically have greater exposure to the mass media, are more cosmopolitan, have greater contact with change agents, have more social experience and exposure, are higher socioeconomic status and are more innovative.

You will be more effective as an Innovation Strategist if you create a network of thought leaders to collaborate with in transforming your organization and making innovation sustainable. That means connecting people from different departments or fields of study, with pertinent information and convincing them to create actionable ideas that produce value.

Thought Leader Networks

Thought leaders can play a major role in the adoption of innovation through their social networks by creating innovation networks. There are a number of examples of successful innovation networks, such as one developed at Proctor and Gamble. Larry Huston, who was vice president of knowledge and innovation for many years there, was the architect of its Connect + Develop program, an approach that helped extend the company's innovation process to include 1.5 million people outside of P&G. [77] He determined that future competitive advantage will depend on "innovation networks" -- individuals and organizations outside a company that can help it solve problems and find new ideas for creating growth.

.The Energy Innovation Networks is an example of a group of entrepreneurs looking for researchers who can develop new technologies; startups to connect with a lead customer; large private sector corporations that seek state policies that make financial sense of investments in renewable energy; states that enact policies that will encourage economic development; and regions that scale state-level innovation strategies. [78]

Another example, the Business Performance Innovation (BPI) Network, is dedicated to identifying, exploring and sharing emerging trends and transformational ideas and practices that are reshaping world markets and competitive landscapes: The BPI Network aims to help senior executives and their multi-national workforces become more inventive, market-centered, operationally efficient, and competitive in a challenged and changing global and local context.[79]

Viral Innovation: Mobile Apps

A recent Harvard Business Review article recommended this concept of making your product intrinsically viral. It suggests that adding a "share" button to a product can increase peer-to-peer influence over product purchase by 400 percent.[80] The article uses the example of a multinational financial institution that embedded its product in SharePoint by including a "share" button for 30,000 internal stakeholders. It instantly became viral and its potential market increased exponentially.

Mobile applications for smartphones are one of the fastest growing segments of the information and computing technology (ICT) industries. According to the analyst firm research2guidance, the mobile application marketplace could grow from a $1.94 billion business in 2009 to a $15.65 billion business in 2013—a growth rate of around 807 percent. The study also predicts the smartphone user base to grow from 100 million to 1 billion in that same time frame. Currently, only 10 percent of the Fortune 2000 is engaging their customer base with a mobile application. The Nielsen Company reported Monday that smartphones now account for 28 percent of the cell phone market in the United States. Nielsen's report also states that 41 percent of cell phones purchased in the U.S. over the past six months were smartphones.[81]

A new report from research firm Canalys indicates that direct revenue from mobile app stores will almost double within the next year to $14.1 billion, a 92 percent rise from an expected $7.3 billion in 2011. Estimates suggest that app store revenue will continue to boom over the next four years, reaching $36.7 billion by 2015, with an expected four-year compound annual growth rate of 50 percent. The rise in application downloads will be facilitated by the strength of the smartphone market, with shipments expected to include 419 million handsets and over 43 million tablet devices in 2011.[82]

Capitalizing on this growing trend, the Institute for Innovation offers the following mobile applications:

- **Trend Search**™ (basic) delivers trends to a subscriber's smartphone. The basic default categories are economic, social-cultural, legal/

regulatory, and technology trends. This requires a free download of the software from their respective application store and a basic monthly subscription.

- **Trend Search Premium**™ uses our bisociation brainstorming® technique to converge two trends to anticipate disruptions and discover opportunities and challenges for their organization or industry. The user's new ideas are entered in a text box and can be sent to a blog moderated by the Institute for Innovation or to the Idea Accelerator™ database.

- **Trend Search Pro**™ allows a thought leader or organization to create a private and secure blog or discussion group for their stakeholders, whether they are employees or clients. The ideas generated from the brainstorming activity from their smartphone can be posted on the blog of the organization or group using our SharePoint for further discussion or innovation activities. With this tool, Innovation Strategists can conduct open ideation forums and open innovation activities. Marketing organizations can identify new market applications. Strategic planning groups can get hierarchically and geographically diverse stakeholder input on key decision-making. Entrepreneurs can use it to brainstorm business model innovations.

These activities can become viral using social media techniques such as "like," "share" or "tweet." Reward systems can track contributions and referrals by user/subscriber for contests or point systems that be applied toward the cost of the application or for intrinsic recognition. Trend Search Premium™ can be used by independent consultants to create their own thought leader group or innovation network. Using a blog or discussion group controlled by invitation only, they can create a knowledge base for intellectual capital development and client development.

As a Certified Innovation Strategist with the Institute for Innovation, you can access the social media feature embedded in our Idea Accelerator™software. Built in Microsoft SharePoint, it has viral-inspiring features such as wiki, discussion boards, chat and networking.

CHAPTER 8

WINNING THE FUTURE:
BEST PRACTICES IN THE PUBLIC
SECTOR

"Strategic planning for the future is the most hopeful indication of our increasing social intelligence."—William Hastie

In our new global economy the race is on for winning the future. Considering the unprecedented and complex challenges facing today's governments at all levels and in all locales around the world, systematized, creative disruption in the service of innovation has never been more essential. The dominance of Western capitalism is at a tipping point. The European Union is weakening due to the weight of unrealistic economic growth by some of its members that has been fueled by an over-reliance on debt. New economic powerhouses such as Brazil, Russia, India, and China (BRIC) are causing a paradigm shift in economic comparative advantage.

Additionally small countries and nation states such as South Korea and Singapore are also emerging by establishing innovation niches in key industries. They have been able to marshal resources such as well-educated human capital in science, technology, engineering, and math (STEM) disciplines. In addition to a skilled workforce what they have in common is a national focus on developing an innovation ecosystem.

This chapter considers best practices in strategic foresight that provides a framework for national and regional public sector innovation initiatives. It illustrates how these organizations can develop and implement best practices that will allow them to create their own highly effective innovation environments in order to win the future. For each example of strategic transformation, I suggest best practices and describe how the Idea Accelerator™ can be a viable solution to address these issues.

Best Practices in Strategic Foresight Studies

I was recently invited to give a keynote address at an International Strategic Foresight Conference[83] held in Brasilia, Brazil, sponsored by the Centro de Gestao e Estudos Estrategicos (Center for Strategic Studies and Management Science, Technology and Innovation), or CGEE. Experts came from Europe, Canada, Asia, South America and the U.S. to present concepts on foresight and innovation.[84] The conference focused on best practices for developing a transformative innovation ecosystem at the national level. I will group these concepts into the categories of knowledge, people, process and technology.

In the knowledge category, the experts suggest the following issues should be considered in developing a best-practice approach to strategic foresight:

- **Knowledge**: Efforts to discover knowledge must evolve from data hunting, management and sharing. Methodology is needed to help foresight specialist change information into strategic intelligence. New knowledge creation must focus more on what we don't know.
- **Cross disciplinary trends**: Knowledge creation can be enhanced by analyzing trends, predictions and emerging issues from varied disciplines and subject areas.
- **Break/Challenge mindset**: Focusing on conventional drivers yields conventional ideas. Find ways to think outside the box using trans-disciplinary knowledge and cross-disciplinary groups.

One of the areas that gained consensus from the panel of experts related to techniques on how to get thought leaders engaged in the strategic foresight process. They suggested the following:

- **Create uneasiness**: Avoid what is comfortable and familiar to achieve innovative foresight.
- **Remarkable people**: Get remarkable people involved to get remarkable results.
- **Appropriate mix**: Get an appropriate mix of people by striving for diversity in terms of ethnicity, gender, occupation, hierarchical status and functional responsibilities.
- **Innocent people**: Involve "innocent people" that are not traditional stakeholders bound by traditional paradigms and thought processes.
- **Creative Competence**: Make creativity a competence by finding ways to stimulate and reward creativity as a valued competence.
- **Preparation**: Prepare participants involved with strategic foresight activities in advance by using psychological tools and assessments.

It is also important to develop a systematic foresight process. Some of the ideas presented included:

- **Methodology**: Brainstorming and foresight activities must be systematic and participatory.
- **Real-time Delphi**: Create an environment with a collaborative technology or platform that allows continued and structured dialogue among subject matter experts.
- **Brainstorm technical applications**: Spend quality time and effort on brainstorming applications for new and old technologies, rather than just research and development of new technology.
- **Transformational foresight**: Focus on foresight activities that have the potential to transform society, economies, technology and organizations.
- **Outside the box thinking**: Use thinking mechanisms that are unconventional to generate unique ideas.

- **Decision Theater**: Provide a platform for making decisions that allows participants to better visualize complexity in a real-time, crowdsourcing environment. This foresight platform should include a databank of knowledge.
- **Social networking**: Use social networking tools to improve interaction and collaboration of thought leaders.
- **Convergence of drivers**: Focus on the intersection of drivers and trends to uncover many permutations of future possibilities.
- **Wildcard scenarios**: Consider the wildcards, but resist becoming preoccupied with the wrong things.
- **Provocative scenarios**: Construct provocative scenarios to stimulate interesting ideas.

The preceding list of ideas creates a strong platform for designing strategic foresight conferences and developing foresight processes. In summary, thought leaders should focus on developing a replicable and sustainable strategic foresight system that does the following:

- Transforms foresight into innovation
- Stimulates imagination and interaction
- Engages people in a way that is systematic and iterative, not random or serendipitous
- Uses visuals and graphics to focus attention on key information
- Collaborates via social networks and crowdsourcing platforms
- Involves the right interdisciplinary people
- Accumulates and shares future-focused knowledge using collaborative technology
- Systematically generates new ideas for technology and application
- Discovers solutions that have major impact on societal challenges
- Provides a roadmap for anticipating emerging business opportunities.

Addressing these points is not really an option these days for public-sector organizations—it is essential for growing and thriving in the years ahead. But what is the best methodology for addressing these? Read on.

Strategic Foresight Conference Planning

A strategic foresight conference is typically organized to explore growth opportunities for a particular sector or industry, as initiated by a government agency or industry association. The output from a foresight study is a macro-level technology or strategic road map for the development of a national or regional economy. This section offers strategies I presented at the International Strategic Foresight Conference as founder of the Institute for Innovation. Our proprietary Idea Accelerator™ electronic brainstorming software facilitates this strategic foresight methodology. Both the methodology and software have been used by CGEE in two previous studies: advanced materials and photovoltaic industries.

Such an effort is most effective when it includes a diverse group of scientists, business leaders and entrepreneurs, policy-makers, and social scientists to brainstorm ideas and solutions to key issues. A first step in planning a strategic foresight conference is to achieve consensus on the priority topic or issue. Appropriate issues may include:

- Improve nation's comparative advantage and trade accounts
- Reduce national deficits
- Improve government efficiency
- Improve regional competitiveness
- Improve technology transfer to commercial sector
- Improve sustainable energy sources
- Improve quality of environment
- Reduce energy consumption
- Create programs and initiatives for improving the quality of life of citizens
- Produce studies and reports for planning agencies
- Explore competitive dynamics of industry

In a typical CGEE study, a project manager develops a plan in response to a request by the Minister of Science and Technology or the Minister of Industry and Commerce (the federal cabinet level of the Brazilian government). Resources from the highest level of the Federal government are directed to strategic foresight projects as a result of the Law of Innovation enacted in 2005. This legislation was designed to bring public officials, academics and business executives together to encourage innovation.

A planning committee is then formed that includes scientists and administrators from non-governmental and quasi-governmental agencies engaged in policy development, monitoring and execution for the sector or industry. These stakeholders are tasked to review the intellectual capital database, identify technical subject matter experts, and collect or develop reports on the sector.

The planning committee conducts an initial Delphi brainstorming session with subject matter experts to identify more specific themes. Survey instruments, literature reviews, and brainstorming sessions are used to dive deeper into topics. Follow-up meetings to the real-time Delphi session are conducted using web conferencing, mind mapping and strategic visioning collaborative tools in a virtual environment. At this point CGEE uses the Collective Intelligence™ methodology for planning the strategic foresight conference, starting with the administrative and planning steps:

Pre-Conference

1. Instruct each plenary session speaker to provide 10 key trends (dynamic knowledge) for the future in an electronic version of power point slides.
2. Input all key trends into the Idea Accelerator™ database.
3. Have the planning committee review and evaluate trends using Idea Accelerator™ software.
4. Produce top trend cards for use in the brainstorming phase of the strategic foresight workshop.

Research Sources:

- Industry reports
- Technology reports
- Foresight studies
- Strategic plans
- Intelligence reports

- Academic journals
- Call for conference papers
- Call for technical proposals
- Conference presentations
- Newspaper and journal articles
- Website
- Blogs
- Newsletters
- Book summaries
- Internal and intranet documents

Conference Set-Up:

1. Participants complete an innovation style assessment tool and receive individual reports on how they typically solve problems.
2. Conference administrators review participant data from the innovation style assessment and form groups to ensure discipline and innovation style diversity.
3. Registrants self-identify their stakeholder group and register for innovation workshops.

Once organized stakeholders are actively engaged by Certified Innovation Strategists from the Institute for Innovation to facilitate a number of brainstorming activities that are detailed as follows:

Strategic Visioning Process:

1. Participants break out into "solutions teams" for each theme. Stakeholder diversity is preferred, particularly from the perspectives of industry sectors and functional areas.
2. A session recorder documents brainstorming ideas using mind mapping software to gain consensus and visualize the issues (see example in figure 5-1).
3. Solution teams use the Idea Accelerator™ methodology to discover opportunities, challenges and innovative ideas using our proprietary trend database and bisociative brainstorming techniques.

Solutions Teams Reporting and Action:

1. Facilitator reports ideas with recommendations.
2. Participants rate ideas and provide comments.
3. Scenarios are written by solution teams and presented at the closing session.
4. Initial road maps are developed to identify gaps in terms of intellectual, human, organizational and financial capital.

Innovation 2.0: A Virtual Think Tank

As a follow up to the Strategic Foresight Conference the Institute for Innovation provides an online crowdsourcing platform for continued interaction of solution teams. We facilitate online collaborative innovation sessions with our team of Certified Innovation Strategists to coach solution teams. Solution teams continue to develop new ideas using our software to expand conference output and the database on trends and public-private business models. Final reports are developed using printouts from the Idea Accelerator™ that summarize all trends, drivers, opportunities, challenges, ideas, scenarios, and evaluative comments that have been identified as part of the solutions.

The International Foresight Conference I have described brought experts together to discuss strategic foresight planning. The Six Steps to Collective Intelligence methodology used in the Idea Accelerator™ software addresses many of the expert's recommendations, demonstrating best practices in planning for transformational innovation. Of course, it would be presumptuous to assume that our methodology addressed all of the subject matter experts' recommendations. Nor do I assume this methodology fits all foresight activities and requirements. Considerable research still needs to done to confirm that the ideas generated could not have been developed using other techniques. For example, future research should address the question of whether bisociation generates higher quality and more comprehensive ideas and solutions. Based on the feedback of the sponsors CGEE plans to use Idea Accelerator in future studies.

These recommendations can also help planning agencies in emerging economies develop a purposeful plan for transformative innovation.

I welcome opportunities for collaboration on implementing a strategic foresight and virtual think tank.

Regional Strategic Foresight

A recent planning engagement with the Institute for Emerging Issues (IEI) demonstrates how a strategic foresight project can accelerate innovation for a regional area. IEI is a think tank whose mission is to engage key decision makers and constituents on key issues in North Carolina. It organizes a statewide conference to ensure North Carolina's future competitiveness. The Institute for Innovation was engaged to help external stakeholders and staff identify key issues for upcoming conferences.

Our pre-planning activities included a teleconference with its Issues Council, which included key thought leaders from four basic areas: education, health, business and the environment. The purpose of the meeting was to identify their initial thoughts about key issues. The key topics are summarized below:

Health

- We cannot "treat" ourselves out of the current health care issues. We need concrete thoughts and policy statements that address prevention.
- Obesity is a very big problem and people need to know the importance of taking care of themselves.
- We need to invest in Electronic Health Records-especially in rural communities
- Smaller rural communities are suffering. The job market is down, income is down, and physicians do not want to live in these communities

Education
- Key issues in K-12: Parental engagement, teacher/principal engagement and retention, kindergarten readiness, end of 3rd grade achievement
- Culture change: We need to expect more of students and set higher standards
- Graduation rates for four-year universities must be raised

- Lifelong learning is essential and must include issues of equitable access and expanding broadband coverage/usage

Environment

- Climate change and community adaptation strategies. We need sensible actions in the face of the risk of uncertainty when infrastructure investments could be impacted.
- We need financing for the enormous infrastructure improvements that are needed, especially for the many small water and wastewater systems.
- Public policy at the state level needs to be tailored to the unique needs and circumstances of different regions of the state (urban, rural, coast, mountains, etc.). Different regions have different needs and assets that relate to economic development, environmental protection, public financing, energy policy, and land use planning.
- Development of a green energy economy has great potential in North Carolina if barriers are removed.

Economy

- Substantial and repeated across-the-board budget cuts are not optimal in terms of positioning the state for future growth and development. Rather, the budget situation is an opportunity to rethink and reallocate resources in new directions. Specific suggestions include eliminating overlap within the economic development system and focusing on new strategies to grow the economy and wages.
- The state's funding challenges offer an opportunity to rethink how we "do" higher education in NC
- The community colleges are the fastest growing educational entity in the state; however, they receive the lowest per-student funding. This issue must be addressed.
- We need a discussion about which services citizen's want and how to provide and pay for them, i.e. the mix of public, public, public-private delivery mechanisms that might be employed.

- How can the state best help those elements of the population—middle aged, lacking current skills, dislocated from previous jobs and careers—that are finding it hard to reengage in the workforce at a time when wages for low skilled labor are falling?

Exploring Regional Trends

The initial thoughts generated at the conference were then provided to the staff of IEI to conduct research on trends that relate to each of the topics. A sampling of the trends discovered in each category is as follows:

What is a new and/or important issue impacting the issue area?	**TECHNOLOGY:** Role of technology/ transition to digital world/access to information
What are the major changes/ trends on this issue in the past several years?	• There has been an increase in the use of technology (e.g. smartphones) that allows youth to be constantly "plugged in" - 1/3 of youth today now own a smartphone. Among 18-24 year olds, Internet use is heavily affected by whether or not they attend school or college. Among those in school or college, 85 percent use the Internet, compared to 51.5 percent of those who are not in school.

What is a new and/or important issue impacting the issue area?	HEALTH: Obesity
What are the major changes/ trends on this issue in the past several years?	• 57 percent all North Carolinians are either overweight or obese, up 82 percent from 1990-2002. Further, 26 percent of youth 12-18 and 20 percent of children 5-11 are overweight or obese. This is significantly higher than the national average. • Younger students report higher rates of overweight and obesity. While not statistically significant, the number of obese high school students has increased from 12.8 percent to 13.4 percent (2001-2009). • Minorities are more likely to experience overweight and obesity than white residents.

What is a new and/or important issue impacting the issue area?	ECONOMIC: Participation in the global economy
What are the major changes/ trends on this issue in the past several years?	• While domestic economic growth may be slow, some markets abroad are doing quite well and provide opportunity for exports. From 2009 to 2010, North Carolina exports increased by 14 percent, even as the larger state economy sputtered. • North Carolina increasingly is perceived as an attractive place for foreign investment. FDI Magazine ranked Charlotte and Greenville in the top five cities (in their respective population categories) in the Western Hemisphere for their ability to attract foreign direct investment.

What are the major changes/trends on this issue in the past several years?	• This is an ongoing issue that has not been solved. North Carolina's water challenges are many - conflicts between users rely on individual lawsuits, very few places in the state can build new reservoirs, and regulation makes it difficult to move large quantities of water from one basin to another. With North Carolina poised to become the 7th largest state by 2030, measures must be put in place to guard against future shortages; yet once a drought passes, the focusing event is gone from the minds of the North Carolina legislature. • North Carolina has historically relied on rainfall to solve its water supply problems, but we have failed as a state to develop comprehensive water policy despite having severe droughts in the years 2000-2002 and 2007-2008. These droughts, however, along with rapidly increasing conflicts within and among states in the southeastern United States, have begun to move public and political attention to the need for changes in water policy.

Using these trends, Institute for Innovation and IEI staff summarized the top trends on dynamic knowledge cards.

Because of time constraints, the first step of the Idea Accelerator™ methodology was skipped. We started the session by mapping the issues that have been presented to see if there were any other critical areas to consider. The few issues that were added were formatted as trends and added to the Dynamic Knowledge.

The group met and brainstormed opportunities and challenges. The goal was to discover at least six future outcome possibilities. Once each group reached the target, we reconvened to report. This engagement was unique because it was limited to only identifying opportunities and challenges to arrive at a consensus on the most critical issues for the theme of future Issues Forums for consideration by the IEI staff and Board of Directors.

Engaging the Business Community

During the brainstorming process it became obvious that one of the most critical areas to address was how to engage the business community in solving the environmental, health and education issues that could contribute to a prosperous and sustainable economy for the State of North Carolina. This goal later became the subject of another project for the business leaders: how to help organizations develop sustainable corporate social responsibility initiatives.

Corporate Social Responsibility (CSR) is an area that addresses how the commercial sector can improve its impact on the environment, consumers, employees, communities and other external stakeholders. Historical emphasis on philanthropic activities has not proven sustainable because it does not build on the skills of the local communities.

Another approach to CSR is to incorporate a CSR strategy into the business model of the organization. In this vein, Michael Porter, a leading management professor from Harvard, has popularized a concept called Creating Shared Value (CSV).[85] This approach focuses on the opportunities for competitive advantage that come from building a social value proposition into corporate strategy. The next chapter presents a strategic visioning project that targets how to use the Collective Intelligence ™ methodology to develop a CSR project for the commercial sector to improve the competiveness of the North Carolina business community and the quality of life of its citizens.

CHAPTER 9

WINNING THE FUTURE:

BEST PRACTICES IN THE

COMMERCIAL SECTOR

"Technology feeds on itself. Technology makes more
technology possible."

—Alvin Toffler, Future Shock

Technology Disruption

Major disruptions in the future will be caused by the creation of
breakthrough technology, just as they have been in the past. One of the
most significant technology disruptions of the past decades has been
the Internet. Although the Internet existed with early networks such as
Gopher and FidoNet, the development of the web browser as a business
method patent made the Internet user friendly and more accessible. As
the Internet evolved and became ubiquitous and universally accessible, it
eventually became a great disruptor in commerce.

This evolution of e-commerce fostered the dot.com frenzy of the late
1990s. Considerable wealth was created based on intangible assets and
speculation; value was not measured in terms of profit or tangible assets.
Amazon, for example, experienced tremendous growth in value over
several years in the 1990s before making a profit. The Internet technology

provided opportunity for value creation through web-based Business Model Innovation.

There are a number of areas of technology that can be the source of major disruption in the future. I predict that the next big wave for technology that will be in clean and renewable energy. Whichever country or corporation creates a major disruption in this area will have significant opportunities for wealth creation. Some of this technology is percolating in universities and labs all over the world, whether in wind, solar, bio-fuels, or enabling technologies such as superconductivity or cold fusion. The process of bringing the theoretical and basic research to market, particularly from resources such universities and non-profit science laboratories is called "technology commercialization."

Technology commercialization is an important application of innovation that involves the evolution of technology and products from the R&D lab of your organization and into the marketplace for sale. This chapter discusses how our innovation system can be applied to converting new technology and products into viable business opportunities. One of the examples I will use is the technology transfer process used by research based universities and corporate laboratories.

Technology Commercialization

The Carnegie Foundation for the Advancement of Teaching designates most major universities that conduct theoretical and applied science in the United States as Doctoral/Research Universities Extensive. These are institutions that focus heavily on research in addition to their teaching mission. The university typically owns the intellectual capital developed by academic staff during their employment.

To provide incentives and support for academics in their efforts to realize an economic reward beyond the salaries and bonuses associated with grants and publications, most universities have staff dedicated to the technology transfer of intellectual capital to the commercial sectors. The university takes ownership of the intellectual property and contracts with the scientist, licenses the rights to the product to entrepreneurs, and pay royalties back to the scientist.

There are three basic business models used in the case of technology commercialization:

- The Vertical Model develops a technology platform and licenses it out.
- The Platform Model focuses on developing a product and selling it yourself or licensing the rights.
- The Product Model 'generates revenue at all levels of product development, from early concept to the marketing stage. There has been a decline in the use of the Product Model because of its inherent risks associated with the early stage of development and commercialization.

In all cases, patents and intellectual property (IP) are at the core of value creation. But in the lean times we have experienced since the financial market collapse, the Platform Model has become a favorite model for mitigating risk. As venture capital sources become more available, the Product Model could become more accessible.

I have attended a number of events sponsored by the major U.S. based industry association in this field, the Association of University Technology Managers (AUTM). Many of its members are focused on the contractual issues of patents, licensing and royalty payments. The technology transfer officers at universities typically manage a portfolio of very interesting technologies, but do not spend a lot of time focused on innovation. In other words, they have not spent a great deal of energy on how to make money from their technology development. Their typical approach is to hope that an entrepreneur, leading a venture capitalist by the hand, comes to claim the market virtues of the technology of their professors and scientists. Unfortunately, this serendipitous meeting of the minds does not happen often enough to accelerate innovation.

After attending a regional meeting of AUTM, I was invited to a major university in the southern part of the U.S. to propose a commercialization seminar that would bring entrepreneurs and scientists together to brainstorm market applications for their technology portfolio. They were more interested in how to execute the administrative and contractual aspects of licensing and royalty payments, and the notion of ideation was not a priority.

As discussed throughout the pages of this book, I see creative disruption as a proactive approach to discovering new applications for technology. By intentionally creating disruption through the commercialization of technology, economic value can be generated that will benefit all stakeholders, including funding for scientific exploration and wealth for investors.

Technology Opportunity Workshop

One of the most important challenges facing any economy is the development of the entrepreneurial sector through commercialization of technology. In the United States 60 percent of jobs created each year are created by small enterprises. In fact, making sure the innovation renaissance inspires entrepreneurship is a particular focus of the book.

To be proactive I suggest using our Six Step Collective Intelligence system and tools to organize a technology commercialization opportunity fair. The call to action below is a guide used by a typical conference to invite entrepreneurs, investors and scientists to brainstorm technology applications.

Call to Action

Technology Opportunity Workshop

1. Conference organizers invite a specific number of technology teams.
2. They are allowed a 10-minute presentation on the layman's version of their technology.
3. Using the Six Step Collective Intelligence methodology, the scientists, entrepreneurs and investors are allowed 30 minutes to brainstorm applications. The bisociation brainstorming process typically holds the technology variable constant and considers several combinations of economic, social, and regulatory trends to discover future possibilities. As an alternative, the entrepreneurs could use trends from their specific industrial sector, such as health, education, transportation, etc.

A typical visioning session for a technology commercialization project would involve choosing a particular technology trend and holding it as the constant while considering the interactions with other trends. Using this brainstorming approach, there should be a limitless supply of opportunities for new ventures.

Technology Transfer: A Case Study

One of my first projects using the Six Step Collective Intelligence was a technology commercialization workshop with the University of North Carolina, Wilmington, which has a Ph.D. program in marine science. These "entrepreneurial scientists," as we called them, worked on marine science research during the day and took MBA classes at night. In the second year of the MBA, curriculum students engage in a practicum that involves developing a business or technology commercialization plan. To accelerate their focus on applications for their research, we conducted a commercialization seminar. The participants included marine science faculty, business faculty, and the post doc students.

To jumpstart the brainstorming process, the Institute for Innovation contracted with a research group to develop trends for the participants to use. One of the early lessons from this experience was in order for the bisociation brainstorming process to be more effective, the trends needed to be unrelated. In this case the researchers found all trends related to marine science, differing only in terms of the technology, economic regulation or social aspects of marine science. As a result, when the trends were converged during the brainstorming, most of the opportunities and challenges discovered were not very sensational. Most bordered on possibilities that the scientist had considered to some degree.

But, all was not lost in the exercise. One opportunity discovered led to a new idea for one of the student's technology. An application for a fish farm was discovered and became the topic of the student's business plan. Subsequent development included filing a patent for the development of a prototype and the initiation of a new venture to market the product.

Corporate Social Responsibility: A Case Study

As a result of the strategic foresight project previously mentioned in the previous chapter, the Institute for Innovation designed a blueprint for developing a corporate sustainability strategy that could be used by commercial sector companies in the region. Corporate social responsibility (CSR) is part of an emerging trend for organizations to make environmental and social impact on their internal and external stakeholders an important part of their mission.

Social responsibility is the expectation that business will strive to improve the overall welfare of society. A study by Cone Communication found that 84% of American say they would likely switch brands to one associated with a good cause, if price and quality are similar.[86] A Hill and Knowlton/Harris's Interactive poll revealed that 79% of Americans take corporate citizenship into account in buying decisions. [87] An Accenture report suggests that the goals of sustainability and profitability are mutually exclusive. In this study CEOs indicated that the recent recession only heightened the importance of sustainability.[88]

Michael Porter, one of the leading authorities in management, recently introduced the concept of "Shared Value" in a Harvard Business Review article.[89] This perspective suggests that the purpose of the corporation is to create shared value not just profit. This means advancing the economic as well as the social conditions in the environments in which firms operate. He claims this will drive the next wave of innovation and productivity growth in the global economy.

One example of a contrasting approach to the shared value concept is fair trade, which attempts to increase the proportion of revenue that goes to poor farmers through redistribution. Shared value, on the other hand focuses on improving growing techniques that could increase efficiency and crop yields, product quality and sustainability.

In addition to the traditional business goal of maximizing shareholder wealth, this triple-bottom-line strategy, also called corporate sustainability, focuses on sustaining the environment. A CSR strategy provides an opportunity for developing intellectual property for commercializing clean technology. It considers sustainable community development by looking at the social needs and quality of life for the communities of its employees, customers, and communities from a local and a global perspective. I address the social transformation part of this mission in the next chapter.

We have also used the Six Step Collective Intelligence methodology to develop a strategic foresight conference on corporate social responsibility focused on sustainable energy. The plan is designed as a 1 ½-day strategic retreat for leaders from diverse sectors of the economy. The participating organizations dedicate managers to take the Certified Innovation Strategist (CIS) course, which is a "train the trainer" curriculum to become qualified as team leaders for the conference. We use the CIS training as the planning phase for the conference

As a starting point of Phase 1 we use the six CSR domains identified in a study done by Price Waterhouse Cooper (PWC).[90] Using this matrix and the participants develop a mind map for visualizing the strategic knowledge related to these basic domains of CSR activities.

	Management System	Environment	Supply Chain	Employees	Health & Safety	Community Support
Cost savings and productivity	✓					
Energy usage in raw materials, supplies transportation		✓				
Improving supplier status			✓			
Investment attractiveness				✓		
Product/ service innovation	✓					

Employee recruitment					✓	✓
Regulation compliance	✓					

Figure 9-1: The Corporate Social Responsibility matrix is a starting point for visioning.

The environmental scanning phase focuses on dynamic knowledge research (trends, emerging issues, and expert predictions) to identify changes in the industry related to supply chain activities, processes, and products. In a newsletter produced by Environment Leader[91] some of the trends predicted for 2011 include:

1. The embedding of sustainability as a core business strategy
2. Establishment of a consensus on the role of the sustainable development professional
3. The rise of the Chief Sustainability Officer
4. Increased transparency, an open society and a decrease in green washing
5. Supply chain engagement, where supplier's performance is also monitored and reported on, forming part of the corporate sustainability strategy.
6. IT for green purposes growing at an exponential rate

For future projects we will use the Trend Search mobile application at this stage to get the participants engaged in familiarizing themselves with trends and the process of connecting the dots (trends) prior to the conference.

In Phase 2 participants are asked to complete the Innovation Style Assessment prior to coming to the opening session of the CSR Visioning Retreat. Upon arrival they are given color-coded badges that indicates their innovation style and profile, to use as an icebreaker. The purpose of the exercise is also to get participants to reflect on and articulate their innovation and problem solving style.

Participants are divided into "solution teams" of eight, including the team leader, based on diverse innovation profiles and functional disciplines. The solution teams are assigned one of three themes: supply chain, product development or internal process. The session starts by reviewing the mind map developed by the project leaders (Step 2). Any additions to the themes, objectives, and functions are noted. Each group is provided with 20 trends that were developed by the project leaders in Phase 1 training.

A brainstorming exercise engages participants in the experience of building three dimensional structures by attaching cards to square cardboard boxes with the DK cards for bisociating on the first level, the opportunity/challenge cards for bisociating with business models on the second level, and new ideas cards on the third level. Groups are encouraged to be creative by building on a broad base of many trends, like the Great Wall of China, or a skyscraper structure that uses limited trends to create many opportunities and ideas, stacked on top of each other in layers.

To create a scenario based on the ideas developed by the group they are asked to create a screenplay to illustrate the impact of the new idea. They also produce a Strategic Foresight Roadmap that identifies the gaps that need to be addressed in technology, markets, human resources and infrastructure.

To conclude this exercise the groups are asked to develop metrics that can be used to set up the Business Model Innovation Scorecard with benchmarks for measuring success. The new ideas are used to develop a new value proposition to articulate how organizations can create value using a CSR strategy. This example of the CSR Visioning project provides a best practice for using the Six Step Collective Intelligence™ methodology to brainstorm ideas on improving an organization's environmental impact that can apply to a very broad group of industries.

CHAPTER 10

WINNING THE FUTURE:

CREATING DISRUPTION IN THE

SOCIAL SECTOR

"Philanthropy is commendable, but it must not cause the philanthropist to overlook the circumstances of economic injustice which make philanthropy necessary."—Martin Luther King, Jr.

The Need for Social Transformation

There has been an alarming trend in increasing income inequality in the United States of America. According to a United States Department of Commerce and Internal Revenue Service study in 2011 the top 1 percent of households gained about 275 percent between 1979 and 2007.[92] In fact as of 2006, the U.S. had one of the highest levels of income inequality, as measured through the Gini index.[93] The US is one of only a few developed countries in which income inequality has increased since 1980. Some would suggest that this trend has been the catalyst for the "Occupy" Movement of 2011.

The wealth gap between Caucasians and African Americans today is the widest it has been in the last 25 years, according to a new study by the Congressional Budget Office in 2011.[94] Caucasians have an average wealth 20 times greater than African Americans and 18 times greater than Hispanics. For African Americans African Americans this represents a sharp increase from the 12 to 1 gap in the 1980s. The widening of this gap is largely due to the decline of home values and the greater disparity in unemployment during the recent recession. African Americans have the highest unemployment rate of all groups, reaching 16.2 percent in 2011.

As wonderful as capitalism is as an economic system, free market activities do not eliminate structural inequalities in society. These inequalities are not always the result of the "survival of the fittest" theories that assume reward and success are in direct proportion to hard work. All people are not on the proverbial level playing field assumed in Adam Smith's model of market forces. Whether you were born in a geographic area riddled with civil strife, drought, earthquakes, or tsunamis, or faced with catastrophic health failures that can drain resources and impair your ability to work, we do not all have equal advantages and opportunities.

That is why the social sector provides a safety net for under privileged, under resourced, or historically discriminated against groups or individuals. And the need for innovation is just as critical in the social sector as it is in the commercial sector, particularly in those areas with the most social enterprise activity. Each of these areas has significant dynamics of change driving emerging issues that create disruptions:

- Low income and affordable housing
- Access to food and clean water
- Health and nutrition disparities
- Access to quality education and affordable child care
- Renewable energy and ecological sustainability
- Social justice
- Economic empowerment and economic inclusion
- Workforce development
- Arts/culture

Corporate social responsibility as discussed in the previous chapter addresses these needs from the perspective that businesses will strive to improve the overall welfare of society.

Howard Rasheed, Ph.D.

Social Disruption in the Gulf Coast: A Case Study

How do you apply business principles to social transformation? Some lessons can be gained from a case study that evolved from my work helping produce a blueprint for social and economic development along the Gulf of Mexico. The unique context of this engagement is the natural and man-made disasters that have hit the region, from Hurricanes Ivan (2004), Katrina (2005), and Rita (2005), to the BP drilling platform explosion and oil spill in 2010. This series of events has left emotional as well as economic scars that will take years to repair.

In response to these disasters, a regional conference called Regional Equity to Achieve Prosperity (REAP) was convened by Ibis Partners Community Development Corporation in August 2011. The REAP pre-planning session hosted by Ibis Partners in March 2011 brought together some of the sponsors and organizers in Pensacola, Florida. The first phase of the planning session for the summit involved several Gulf Coast agencies, including the Bay Area Chamber of Commerce, the Pensacola-Escambia Human Relations Commission, and Gulf Power, the regional utility company. Other agencies included the Gulf Coast Fund, a grant making intermediary that awarded $5 million to more than 200 agencies in the 2010 fiscal year; and the Maritime Park, a multi-use residential, commercial, and athletic waterfront development in downtown Pensacola. This public-private sector project has used Community Benefit Agreements to ensure inclusion by historically underutilized sections of the community.

As consultants we engaged the participants in a mind mapping exercise that focused on the following areas:

- Economic and business development
- Health and human services
- Housing
- Education and workforce development

Using the bisociative brainstorming process we cited trends from each category to identify potential future disruptions in terms of opportunities and challenges. They included:

1. The need for affordable housing will increase due to federal and state budget cutbacks expected to the Community Block Grant Fund program.
2. Government funding cuts to pre-kindergarten programs, especially Head Start.
3. Ecological damage from Hurricanes Ivan, Katrina, and Rita, as well as the BP oil spill, has increased in the past seven years.
4. An increase in allocating local school board budgets toward charter schools.

We then came up with the following opportunities:

- Explore the possibilities of using the L3C business model to develop a social venture intermediary focused on attracting social mission investments from private foundations to be directed to key targeted industries. This intermediary would provide the financial and programmatic due diligence and technical assistance to grantees on behalf of private foundations. It would also facilitate government grants for workforce training and enable the acquisition of private equity investments for entrepreneurial development.
- Create micro-grid projects that will provide a sustainable energy source for affordable housing projects.
- Identify a new business model for education that could strengthen schools, particularly the pre-k schools that are in jeopardy.

The L3C Hybrid Social Business Model

At the conference I made a presentation on the emerging hybrid business model for social enterprises call the "low-profit limited liability corporation (L3C)." This version of the LLC is a recent legislative offering in several states designed to provide a legal vehicle for social enterprises to accomplish a multiple bottom-line strategy that can attract program related investments (PRI) from private foundations.

A number of new initiatives were birth at the conference. One in particular is the Oasis Plan. This initiative focuses on sustainability issues along the Gulf Coast such as: green business development; organic food; food desert;

holistic healthcare; and community development economic development; and education.

The L3C is designed to apply business principles to social missions and the retention of marginal industries for social benefit and community economic development. Its great potential lies in its ability to operate as a for-profit and accomplish the social mission of a non profit and tax exempt organization. This is particularly critical in the face of looming federal and state budget deficits that will result in a major decline in social funding.

It allows for the following:

- The ability to raise equity capital that is not available to non-profits
- Subordinated and multi-tier equity investment structures
- Subordination of debt capital
- Flexible ownership structures as memberships with unique voting rights, tax benefits, and income distributions
- Access to program related investments from foundations in addition to grants, without private rulings from the IRS
- Joint ventures with tax exempt, non profits, and for profit entities
- Private inurnment incentives for market driven investments
- Social enterprises to replicate scalable business models

Social Venture Intermediary

The social venture intermediary model is similar to the private equity fund model. A private equity fund takes capital from pension funds and other large investor to buy companies as leveraged buyouts. Private-equity funds look for ways to increase the growth of the business as well as cutting costs. Private-equity funds receive an annual management fee of usually 1.5 percent per year and typically receive 20 percent of the profit of their investments only if their investors earn a hurdle rate of at least an 8 percent annual return.

In this case the capital is committed by investments from private foundations. The performance is not expected to yield high returns expected in the standard capital markets. The deals are required to have primarily a social benefit.

A feasibility assessment process could be used to vet some of the potential projects that could from a social venture intermediary project. The following is an outline for a feasibility study to assess needs and opportunities for social transformation using an L3C model.

Call to Action

Sample L3C Feasibility Assessment

These are some aspects to consider for inclusion (with recommended length guidelines):

1. What is the social problem that your organizational will address? Describe the context of the problem. (1 page)
2. How will your organization address, manage or solve the problem? (1 page)
3. How is your solution different than what's already out there? You need to compare it to at least four alternative organizations also trying to address the problem. (2-4 pages)
4. What organizational form (e.g. non-profit, foundation, government, NGO, for-profit, partnership organization, hybrid) is the best for your organization and why? (1 page)
5. Who will benefit from your organization? Include not only people directly affected by the service or product, but the wider society as well. An example: Better education not only helps students in the short term, but affects their work life, earning potential, family's standard of living, and community contributions over the course of their lifetime. (1 page)
6. Who might feel threatened by your organization? This may include direct competitors, organizations affected by your solution, advocacy or lobbying groups, etc. (1-3 pages)
7. How might your organization be funded? (1 page)
8. What potential unintended consequences might your solution cause? (1-2 pages)
9. How are you going to mitigate the risks inherent in your solution related to direct competitors, funding, threats, and unintended consequences?

It is time to be proactive and create a disruption before millions of children fall deeper into the chasm of poverty and illiteracy. For this reason we use education as a best practice example to explore L3C opportunities in greater depth. The question that arises is how to apply the hybrid social venture model to education at pre-k, k-12 and post-secondary levels. More importantly, will it improve the quality and efficiency of education, particularly for the under-resourced segments of society?

Creating Disruptions in Education

A significant emerging issue is the current budget crisis affecting state and federal funding. This disruption will impact the quality of education offerings and the outcomes for a well-educated workforce as the level of global competition continues to rise. The following trends are pertinent to the discussion and contribute to the sense of urgency:

- American scores in math and science have declined compared to other industrialized nations.
- The percentage of students that are not performing at or above grade level has increased among under-resourced and ethnic minority populations.
- The percentage of students dropping out of school has increased among under-resourced and ethnic minority populations.
- Funding for education has declined as a percentage of state and federal budgets.

The debate rages about whether the current paradigm of education needs to be tweaked or transformed. On one side of the debate, supporters of public schools argue that reducing scarce resources would decimate a declining system of education and further disenfranchise minorities and the poor who are economically trapped in under-resourced school districts. They suggest reallocation of resources to address the disparities, such as better pay for teachers in challenging environments and more remedial support to poor performing schools.

The other side of the debate suggests that market conditions will reward the good schools, teachers, and administrators to improve results. The current system of union protectionism and tenure sometimes rewards mediocrity. Should parents of under-resourced students in low-income areas have to rely on a lottery system to gain admittance to a few high quality magnet or charter schools? Should taxpayers provide vouchers to pay for better quality education in non-public schools? Based on the No

Child Left Behind Legislation of the U.S. Department of Education, poor performing schools will be forced to improve or perish.

This debate will escalate with the degree of scarcity the American public is facing in a more globally competitive environment for talent, skills, and markets. As jobs are outsourced because of the global democratization of information and talent, it creates a vicious cycle. Jobs are exported, foreign companies thrive, government revenues decline, investments in education decline, educational performance and companies outsource their skilled positions, etc. Do we continue on this downward spiral or do we intentionally create a disruption in the system? Do we find new models and solutions or continue a debate filled with frustration?

The Emerging Disruption in Head Start

I was invited to Congress in 2011 as a member of a contingent of community leaders by a coalition of organizations spearheaded by the Children's Defense Fund. Two icons in the struggle led our delegation for social justice and educational reform: Marion Wright Edelman and Jeffrey Canada. The purpose of the trip was to lobby senators to save social programs such as Head Start. Head Start, a program of the U.S. Department of Health and Human Services, promotes school readiness by enhancing the social and cognitive development of children by providing educational, health, nutritional, social, and other services.

As that time, the proposed budget cuts could have resulted in a 20 percent decrease in funding of $1.2 billion, 100,000 fewer children serviced and 20,000 jobs lost. This funding cut would have had a devastating effect on a program with proven results for bridging the achievement gap for ethnic minorities and those that subsist near the poverty level. To say this would be a disruption in society, particularly for the most disadvantaged segments, would be an understatement.

The urgency of this disruption was obvious with the looming budget deficits and the ominous cloud of default if the debt ceiling was not raised. Using Strategy Two—Intentionally Creating Disruption—we developed an idea that was almost unthinkable to the entrenched stakeholders in the Head Start industry. Why not privatize Head Start, or at least create a public-private partnership similar to the charter school model in the K-12 school systems?

Establishing an L3C for pre-k education could be a viable solution. First, pre-k is not the responsibility of the public school districts. It is usually managed by a non profit, community based agency with funding from the U.S. Department of Education and local government. Why not create an L3C for-profit entity based on best practices of Head Start and other private models such as Kinder Care and Montessori? This entity could attract investment money from private foundations interested in education such as the Bill and Melinda Gates Foundation and the Walton Family Foundation.

Because of my work in developing a charter school accreditation model for the 100 Black Men of America, I had the opportunity to float the idea among senior program officers at private foundations. The concept was embraced as a good idea since research indicates that jeopardizing pre-k in disadvantaged neighborhoods could set back progress to closing the achievement gap significantly. But it is such a new and emerging potential disruption to education reform and quality improvement that we are not yet on the radar of foundation executives. What is needed is to develop an L3C business model to address the need to include Pre-K.

The beginning of the disruption is already being phased in. Over the next three years, some grantees will be required to re-compete for continued funding. All 1,600 Head Start grantees will be evaluated against seven quality benchmarks. This has already begun affecting the Head Start program in my hometown of Wilmington, North Carolina. The New Hanover County Community Action gets 55 percent of its $3.5 million annual budget from the federal government, with the remainder coming from state and local governments and private donations. Due to recent changes in the Department of Education funding rules the agency will now have to compete for continued funding that may be severely limited in the future.

So the question remains: will we let one of the most successful programs for bridging the achievement gap for minorities and the poor experience a major setback? Fighting the political fight to hold onto funding will be difficult, at best. As the budget crisis and debt ceiling debate have uncovered the inability of the government and consumers to sustain current spending patterns, something has to give. If entitlement programs, such as Medicare and Social Security, are on the chopping block, Head Start does not have a chance. Especially in light of the automatic budget cuts triggered by the failure of the bipartisan Super Budget Committee in the U.S. Congress.

CONCLUSION

A FUTURE OF INNOVATION

A Business Model for the Future

The previous chapters have provided concepts, systems and best practices that can be used by the Innovation Strategist in the much needed innovation renaissance for the future. In this concluding section I explore the future business model for the Institute for Innovation based on information technology megatrends. Finally, I discuss what the future holds in terms of your career objectives, and suggest how you can develop your skill as an Innovation Strategist based on your role in your organization.

In developing the business model for the Institute for Innovation, I often have been asked whether I have used our brainstorming system to plan the future of my own company. The obvious answer is yes, but *how* I have used it is the more important detail.

To reinvent our own business model we used future focused knowledge from a report published in 2011 *by IBM Tech Trends*.[95] Based on a survey of more than 4,000 IT professionals from 93 countries and 25 industries, this report projects that the most important technology trends of the future will be business analytics, cloud computing, mobile applications and social media. I believe the Institute for Innovation already has innovated a business model that is well positioned at the nexus of these four trends.

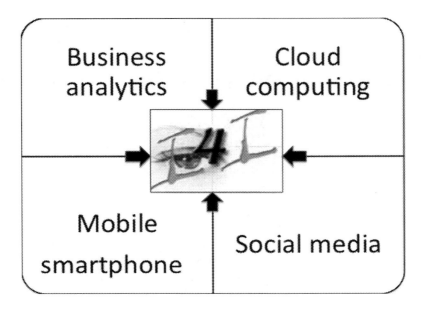

Figure 10-1. The Institute for Innovation is positioning itself at the nexus of these major trends.

According to the report, business analytics is the most adopted technology (90 percent) and shows the least adoption resistance as firms try to automate the process of making sense of vast amounts of data. Additionally, the number of companies using analytics to create a competitive advantage has surged by 57 percent in the past year.

Business analytics involves the skills, technologies, applications and practices for investigating data from past business performance to gain new insight for better decision-making. Business analytics can answer questions such as the following:

- "Why is this happening?"
- "What if the trends continue?"
- "What will happen next?"
- "What is the best (or worst) that can happen?"

This predictive approach is in contrast to a similar area referred to as business intelligence, which looks more simply at what happened, how many, how often, where the problem is and what actions are needed.

Business Intelligence

A new software product under development at the Institute for Innovation combines both business intelligence and business analytics applications. The business intelligence application will automatically search and extract trends, emerging issues and future predictions in diverse knowledge domains from open and secure sources.

Business analytics and artificial intelligence in general has come a long way, as evidenced by the development of IBM Watson, a super computer that was crowned Jeopardy champion. However, while simple facts and predictions based on past data can be processed effectively by super computers, predicting a future that is *not* based on past informational relationships is a much more difficult challenge. It may be 30 to 40 years before artificial intelligence is able to surpass human analysis in this area. Until then, we must rely on human cognitive skills that can be optimized with computer processing, which is exactly our approach at the Institute for Innovation.

The military and intelligence communities are pursuing a methodology for improving the accuracy of forecasting potential conflicts, relying on enhanced contextual awareness through the fusion of diverse hard and soft data. In fact, the U.S. Department of Defense uses a concept called "data fusion" that is the same as our proprietary process of bisociation brainstorming. Using our methodology, we are better able to predict what the military calls Future Outcome Possibilities (FOPs). This leads to optimizing strategic alternatives that the military calls Courses of Action (COAs), but which also can be applied to business analytics.

Mobile Applications

The second area of the IBM study that holds significant potential is mobile computing. Globally, Android and Apple has emerged as the top platforms for mobile application development. In this study 70 percent of respondents are expected to develop applications for the Android platform over the next 24 months, while 49 percent plan to be developed for the Apple operating system.

There is a reason for this: The ability to work effectively from the edges of the network increasingly will be a strategic advantage for any innovation focused organization with a distributed workforce. As indicated in previous chapters, Institute for Innovation has developed a mobile application that can extend our methodology into platforms that are more user-friendly and accessible 24/7.

Cloud Computing

IBM's survey also predicts that cloud computing will continue as a major disrupter in business. This new paradigm encompasses the delivery of Internet-based shared, scalable computing resources, software and information that generally are provided as turnkey solutions rather than individual products. Cloud computing not only offers costs saving on infrastructure, but also allows developers to build and make applications that are available any time and from any location. The vast majority (75 percent) of respondents in the IBM survey believe that over the next two years their organizations will begin to build cloud infrastructure.

The Idea Accelerator™ has been built using a SaaS (Software as a Service) business model. Users do not have to load any software on their host server or computer. All information is entered and accessed remotely through the Institute for Innovation servers. This not only includes access to the brainstorming application, it includes access to the social media features built into the Microsoft SharePoint software platform. These features are part of the social networking technology that corresponds with the social business trend.

Social Media

According to the IBM survey, social business is a clear force in the technical landscape. The much-anticipated Initial Public Offering of Facebook in 2012 is expected to reach $100 billion in value and dramatically illustrates the impact of social media.

A social business model embraces networks of people to create business value by developing a culture of sharing, transparency, innovation, and improved decision making that is critical to innovation. The social business model also enables deeper relationships with value network partners.

According to the survey, the top three goals of social business applications are: employee collaboration, locating people and resources efficiently, and idea generation and sharing. The three top social business capabilities companies utilize are file sharing, blogs and discussion forums. Although many companies are implementing intranet-based solutions in their project initiation, Idea Accelerator™ provides access to these social media features using a cloud-based version of an intranet collaboration platform without buying an additional site license.

This collaboration package of business analytics, cloud computing, mobile application and social media features is obviously a strong business model for winning the future at the Institute for Innovation.

Winning Your Future as an Innovation Strategist

The role of the Innovation Strategist can come in many forms such as entrepreneur, C-level officer, project leader, thought leader or researcher. What is each of these roles and how can what you have learned improve your positioning for the future?

One purpose of this book has been to direct your attention, whether an entrepreneur or executive, to the new frontier of value creation, business model innovation. The traditional thinking has been that intellectual property that creates barriers to entry can only come from breakthrough technology. With the evolution of business method patents, sustainable competitive advantages can be achieved with business model innovations as well. The examples I have shared, such as Google, Priceline, and Amazon, as well as the 2011 patent law changes, illustrate how this new frontier of value creation has changed.

Embracing an Innovation Culture

To succeed in innovation you must build an innovation culture and system with collaborative technology that can become viral for you and your stakeholders. The Six Step Collective Intelligence and the companion Idea Accelerator software provides a blueprint that can be applied to continually reinvent your business model in a way that is attainable for organizations of any size, from small "mom and pop" businesses to the largest corporations and government agencies.

If you're an entrepreneur or running a young business, you may find it very difficult to potentially give up on the technology on which your company may have been built. Keep in mind that stepping back long enough to invest in a new or breakthrough improvement in existing technology and start another innovation life cycle can be daunting, but you really don't have a choice. As I've stated before, if you don't innovate you will perish.

If you're a c-level executive in a larger, established organization, you can move the conversation of innovation beyond R&D and technology to strategic innovation that includes your organization's business model.

Innovation Strategist Positions

The role of Innovation Strategist is to lead an organizational renaissance, whether you are the Chief Executive Officer (CEO) or one of the emerging titles such as Chief Knowledge Officer or Chief Innovation Officer. As the CEO you can set the visionary tone for the organization. The CEO of course can make sure the innovation system has the support and resources necessary to be successful.

The Chief Knowledge Officer (CKO) role is to create, manage, and transform knowledge into intellectual capital or property that creates value in the organization. Knowledge comes in the form of the human capital (people), intellectual capital (processes and product patents) and social capital (stakeholder relationships). The CKO needs to change the paradigm in the organization to focus on dynamic knowledge that can positively impact the future.

A relatively new position is that of the Chief Innovation Officer (CINO). This is a person who not only is responsible for originating new ideas, but also providing systems that enable all the organization's stakeholders to become more creative in transforming opportunities into inventions that lead to innovation. This book should be a guide for the CINO in managing the innovation process to identify strategies, business opportunities, and new technologies. Our innovation ecosystem design should help the CINO develop new capabilities and systems for strategic partners, new business models that can disrupt the industry and create value for the organization.

This book should serve both the CKO and CINO in learning how to collect relevant data that can become useful knowledge for reinventing the future of the organization. They should now have new tools for the development of the knowledge infrastructure. They should be better positioned for facilitating connections in a vibrant innovation ecosystem that has a regenerative culture, replicable system and scalable technology that is contagious. As an Innovation Strategist you can better understand the big picture, become a better advocate for change and better articulate the future of the organization.

If you are a project leader, this book should help you improve the success of your innovation project. Our innovation system should help you improve your abilities in leadership, teamwork and interpersonal skills. You will consequently become a valuable change agent for your organization.

Go Forth and Innovate!

As an Innovation Strategist, you now have the knowledge and tools to better manage an innovation culture, inspire creativity, improve individual learning and enable innovative systems thinking. Implementing reward plans and incentives, providing collaborative technology, and measuring the innovation impact using tools like our Innovation Balance Scorecard for business model innovation, will further improve the success of the organization.

Armed with our strategies and methodology, you now can build an interdisciplinary team of researchers, strategists, technologists and social scientists to optimize your efforts. You can cultivate and engage a pool of experts to aid with ideation; develop relationships with senior client stakeholders, identify strategic goals, manage project teams and client relations. As result you can expect to be successful in winning the future with game-changing ideas.

May you be successful in all the good that you strive for in your attempts to make the future a better place for everyone.

Peace and blessings to you.

ENDNOTES

1 Friedman, Thomas. *The World is Flat*, Farrar, Straus and Giroux, 2005.

2 Crossner, David. *Innovate the Future.* Prentice Hall, 2010.

3 Christensen, Clayton M. *The Innovator's Solution,* Harvard Business Press, 2003

4 Christensen, Clayton M. *The Innovator's Dilemma,* Harvard Business Press, 2003

5 Christensen, Clayton M. Anthony Scott D. and Roth Erik A. *Seeing What's Next: Using the Theories of Innovation to Predict Industry Change* Harvard Business Press, 2004

6 Kern, Frank. "Want: A survey from IBM's Institute for Business Value shows that CEOs value one leadership competency above all others. Can you guess what it is?" *Business Week,* May 18, 2010. Accessed February 2, 2012. http://www.businessweek.com/innovate/content/may2010/id20100517_190221.htm

7 Osterwalder, Alexander. "The Business Model Ontology—A Proposition In A Design Science Approach," PhD dissertation, Universite de Lausanne, 2004.

8 Johnson, Mark Johnson *Seizing the White Space, Business model Innovation for Growth and Renewal*, Harvard Business Press, 2010.

9 Talbert, Marcia Wade. "Discovering the next big idea," *Black Enterprise*, October 2010 Accessed February 2, 2012. http://www.blackenterprise.com/2010/09/30/discovering-the-next-big-idea/

10 Kern, Frank. "Want: A survey from IBM's Institute for Business Value shows that CEOs value one leadership competency above all others. Can you guess what it is?" *Business Week,* May 18, 2010. Accessed February 2, 2012 http://www.businessweek.com/innovate/content/may2010/id20100517_190221.htm

11 Porter, Michael. *Comparative Advantage,* Harvard Press, 1980.

12 The Task Force on the Future of American Innovation, "*The Knowledge Economy: Is the United States Losing Its Competitive Edge? Benchmarks of Our Innovation Future* http://futureofinnovation.org/PDF/Benchmarks.pdf

13 Office of Joseph Lieberman, U.S. Senator. Offshoring Outsourcing and America's Competitive Edge: Losing Out in the High Technology R&D and Services Sector, May 11 2004.

14 Dozm, Y., Wilson, K., Veldhoen, S., Goldbrunner, T., and Altman, G. "Innovation: Is Global the Way Forward?" Booz Allen Hamilton and INSTEAD, 2006. Accessed February 6, 2012. http://www.boozallen. com/media/file/Innovation_Is_Global_The_Way_Forward_v2.pdf

15 Office of Joseph Lieberman, U.S. Senator. Offshoring Outsourcing and America's Competitive Edge: Losing Out in the High Technology R&D and Services Sector, May 11 2004.

16 Friedman, T. *The World is Flat,* Farrar, Straus and Giroux, 2005

17 Mandel, Michael. "Innovation Interrupted", *Business Week*, June 15, 2009.

18 Kao, John. *Innovation Nation*, Free Press, New York, 2007.

19 Mandel, Michael. "Innovation Interrupted", *Business Week*, June 15, 2009.

20 As reported in Star News, Thursday July 28, 2011

21 Safian, Robert. "Generation Flux," *Fast Company*, February 2012, p. 65.

22 Safian, Robert. "Generation Flux," *Fast Company*, February 2012, p. 67-68.

23 Globalization. Accessed March 28, 2012, http://en.wikipedia.org/wiki/ Globalization

24 Sirkin, Harold L. Zinser, Michael, Hohner, D. and Rose, Justin. U.S. Manufacturing Nears the Tipping Point: Which Industries, Why, and How Much? March 22, 2012. Accessed April 8, 2012 www.bcgperspectives. com/content/articles/manufacturing_supply_chain_management_us_ manufacturing_nears_the_tipping_point/

25 Brisson, Zack and Krontiris, Kate. "Tunisia: from revolutions to institutions." The World Bank Group, 2012. Accessed March 25, 2012. http://www.infodev.org/en/Publication.1141.html

26 Hargadon, Arthur. Business Of Innovating: Bringing Low-Carbon Solutions To Market, Pew Foundation Report. October 12, 2011. Accessed March 27. http://www.pewclimate.org/business-innovation/ report

27 Thurow, Lester. *Fortune Favors the Bold: What We Must Do To Build A New And Lasting Global Prosperity*, Harper Collins, 2005.

28 European Commission Foresight Website 2005; FOREN project; FORERA.

29   Bain. Bain Management Tools. Accessed March 28, 2012. http://www.bain.com/Images/Bain_Management_Tools_2011.pdf

30   Koen, P., G. Ajamian, R. Burkart, A. Clamen, J. Davidson, R. D'Amore, C. Elkins, K. Herald, M. Incorvia, A. Johnson, R. Karol, R. Seibert, A. Slavejkov, and K. Wagneret. "Providing clarity and a common language to the 'fuzzy front end'." *Research Technology Management*, 44 no. 2 (2001): 46-55.

31   The 100 Most Creative People in Business, *Fast Company*, www.fastcompany.com/most-creative-people/2011/full-list

32   Chen, M.H., and G. Kaufmann. "Employee Creativity and R&D: A Critical Review," *Creativity & Innovation Management*, 17 no. 1, (2008): 71-76.

33   Rock, David and Schwartz, Jeffrey. "The Neuroscience of Leadership", *strategy+business*, issue 43, 2006

34   Wikipedia. "Six Thinking Hats." Accessed February 6, 2012. http://en.wikipedia.org/wiki/Six_Thinking_Hats

35   Gallupe, R.B., A. Dennis, W.H. Cooper, J.S. Valacich, L.M. Bastianutti, and J.F. Nunamaker, Jr., "Electronic Brainstorming and Group Size" *The Academy of Management Journal*, 35 no. 2, (1992): 350-369.

36   Mueller, Jennifer S., Goncalo, Jack A. Kamdar, Dishan. Recognizing creative leadership: Can creative idea expression negatively related to perceptions of leadership potential? *Journal of Experimental Social Psychology*, 2011.

37   Reported in *Greater Diversity News*, December 1-22, 2010, page 5.

38   Foxall, G.R., and P.M.W. Hackett. "Styles of Managerial Creativity: A Comparison of Adaption-Innovation in the United Kingdom, Australia and the Unites States," *British Journal of Management*, 5 no. 2, (1999): 85-100.

39   Innovation Styles Website. Accessed March 28, 2012. www.innovationstyles.com

40   Fastabend, David A. and Simpson, Robert H. "Adapt or Die: The Imperative for a Culture of Innovation in the United States Army." Accessed March 26, 2012. http://www.au.af.mil/au/awc/awcgate/army/culture_of_innovation.pdf

41   Brinkley, Ian The Knowledge Economy: How Knowledge is Reshaping the Economic Life of Nations, March 2008, as presented at the Innovative People workshop: 18 December 2007, Hosted by the Work Foundation.

42 Brinkley, Ian The Knowledge Economy: How Knowledge is Reshaping the Economic Life of Nations, March 2008, as presented at the Innovative People workshop: 18 December 2007, Hosted by the Work Foundation.

43 Brinkley, Ian The Knowledge Economy: How Knowledge is Reshaping the Economic Life of Nations, March 2008, as presented at the Innovative People workshop:, 18 December 2007, Hosted by the Work Foundation.

44 Brinkley, Ian The Knowledge Economy: How Knowledge is Reshaping the Economic Life of Nations, March 2008, as presented at Innovative People workshop: 18 December 2007, Hosted by the Work Foundation.

45 Wikipedia. "Business Model Innovation." Accessed February 6, 2012. http://en.wikipedia.org/wiki/Business_model_innovation#cite_note-3

46 The Quest for Innovation Management, A Global Study of Global Innovation Management, Amercian Management Association, http://www.amanet.org/images/hri_innovation.pdf

47 Johnson, Mark W. *Seizing the White Space, Business model Innovation for Growth and Renewal*, Harvard Business Press, 2010.

48 Wikipedia. "Business Model Innovation." Accessed February 6, 2012. http://en.wikipedia.org/wiki/Business_model_innovation#citenote-4

49 Osterwalder, Alexander. "The Business Model Ontology—A Proposition In A Design Science Approach," PhD dissertation, Universite de Lausanne, 2004.

50 Watson, Richard. Summary of Trends for 2011. http://toptrends.nowandnext.com/2010/12/20/summary-of-trends-for-2011/

51 Olsen, Stephanie. "Google Lands Web Search Patent," *CNET*, February 5, 2003.
Accessed February 2, 2012. http://news.cnet.com/2100-1024-986204.html

52 Shontell, Alyson. "The 20 Most Innovative Startups in Tech," *Business Insider*, November 8, 2011. Accessed February 2, 2012.
http://www.businessinsider.com/20-innovative-startups-2011-11

53 Fast Company "The World's 50 Most Innovative Companies." Accessed March 26, 12. www.Fastcompany.com/mic/2011

54 Gobry, Pascal-Emmanuel and Carlson, Nicholas. "Is Zynga the most Profitable Company Ever?" *Business Insider*, February 23, 2011. Accessed February 2, 2012.

http://www.businessinsider.com/how-stupid-facebook-games-made-zynga-the-most-profitable-company-ever-2011-2

55 Porter, Michael E., *Competitive Strategy: Techniques for Analyzing Industries and Competitors*. New York: Free Press, 1980.

56 Wikipedia. "Brand." Accessed February 6, 2012. http://en.wikipedia.org/wiki/Brand

57 Cunningham, P. and M. Cunningham (Eds). Collaboration and the Knowledge Economy: Issues, Applications, Case Studies IOS Press, 2008 Amsterdam Business Models for Public Private Partnership: The 3P Framework, http://www.adm.hb.se/~ml/pdf-filer/2008_eChallenges_JHE-ML-OFO-LAL.pdf

58 Combs, David. "State Budget Gaps: How Does Your State Rank?" *Stateline,* March 15, 2011.
Accessed February 6, 2012. http://www.stateline.org/live/ViewPage.action?siteNodeId=136&languageId=1&contentId=15158

59 Jobs, Steve. "The Seed's of Apple Innovation: interview with Steve Jobs." By Peter Burrows. *Business Week,* (October 12, 2004).
http://www.businessweek.com/bwdaily/dnflash/oct2004/nf20041012_4018_PG2_db083.htm

60 Successful Pursuits. "Five Mental Traits of Successful and Innovative People. Accessed February 6, 2012. http://blog.successfulpursuits.com/2009/11/12/five-mental-traits-of-successful-innovative-people/

61 Loewe, P., Williamson, P., and R.C. Wood. "Five Styles of Strategy Innovation and How to use Them" *European Management Journal*, 19 no. 2, (2001): 115-125.
http://blog.successfulpursuits.com/2009/11/12/five-mental-traits-of-successful-innovative-people/

62 Siau, Keng. "Knowledge Discovery as An Aid to Organizational Creativity," *The Journal of Creative Behavior*, 34 no. 4, Fourth Quarter (2000): 248-258.

63 Koestler, Aurthur. (1967). *The Act of Creation: A study of conscious and unconscious in science and art*. Dell Publishing Co.: New York, NY.

64 Ko, Stephen and Butler, John E. "Alertness, Bisociative Thinking Ability, and Discovery of Entrepreneurial Opportunities in Asian Hi-Tech Firms", Babson College, Babson Kauffman Entrepreneurship Research, 2003.

65 Fast Company Staff. "The World's 50 Most Innovative Companies," *Fast Company*, March 2011.

66   Gobry, Pascal-Emmanuel and Nicholas Carlson. "Is Zynga the most Profitable Company Ever?" *Business Insider*, February 23, 2011. Accessed February 2, 2012.
http://www.businessinsider.com/how-stupid-facebook-games-made-zynga-the-most-profitable-company-ever-2011-2

67   Sawyer, Robert Keith. *Group Genius: The Creative Power of Collaboration.* New York: Basic Books, 2007.

68   Ralston, Bill and Wilson, Ian *The Scenario Planning Handbook: Developing Strategies in Uncertain Times;.* Thomson-south-Western; 2006.

69   Gloor, Peter *Swarm Creativity: Competitive Advantage Through Collaborative Innovation Networks.*

70   The Symbiotic Intelligence Project, Accessed April 18, 2012. http://www.collectivescience.com/SymIntel.html

71   Wikipedia. "Open Innovation." Accessed February 6, 2012.
http://en.wikipedia.org/wiki/Open_innovation#cite_note-1

72   "Crowd-sourcing brain research makes big gain". New York Times News Service, as reported in the Wilmington StarNews, April 12, 2012.

73   Brown, Scott, U.S. Senator Website: Accessed March 24, 2012. http://www.scottbrown.senate.gov/public/index.cfm/2012/3/sens-scott-brown-merkley-bennet-introduce-bipartisan-crowdfund-act

74   Triple Pundit Website. Accessed March 23, 2012. http://www.triplepundit.com/2012/03/senate-bill-passage-crowdfunding-on-horizon/comment-page-1/

75   Gladwell, Malcolm. *The Tipping Point.* Little Brown and Company, 2000.

76   Ahonen, Kasper, and Melkko, 3G Marketing in 2004. Total Telecom in February 2005.

77   Huston, Larry. "Innovation Networks: Looking for Ideas Outside the Company: Interview with Larry Huston." By Knowledge@Wharton. *Innovation and Entrepreneurship*, (November, 14, 2007).
http://knowledge.wharton.upenn.edu/article.cfm?articleid=1837

78   Kauffman The Foundation of Entrepreneurship, The Energy Network. Accessed March 21, 2012. www.energyinnovationnetwork.org.

79   The Business Performance Innovation Network, Accessed March 21, 2012. http://www.bpinetwork.org/

80   Cox, David. S. "Forget Viral Marketing—Make the Product Itself Viral," *Harvard Business Review*, June 8, 2011.

[81] Epstein, Zach. "Nielsen: smartphones now 28% of U.S. cell phone market," Nielsonwire, November 1, 2010. http://www.bgr.com/2010/11/02/nielsen-smartphones-now-28-of-u-s-cell-phone-market/

[82] Brian, Matt. Mobile App market to generate $14.1 Billion revenue next year. Accessed March 26, 20112. http://thenextweb.com/mobile/2011/06/29/mobile-app-market-to-generate-14-1bn-revenues-next-year/

[83] Foresight International Seminar: From Theory to Practice, sponsored by Centro de Gestao e Estudos Estrategicos (CGEE), Brasilia, Brazil, December, 16-17, 2010.

[84] Comments are referenced from the following presentations:

- Filho, Lélio F., Nehme, Claudio Chauke, Santos, Marcio de M. "Language and communication styles required to address the interests and expectations of the client and involved stakeholder: The CGEE Experience." Presentation at Foresight International Seminar: From Theory to Practice, sponsored by Centro de Gestao e Estudos Estrategicos (CGEE), Brasilia, Brazil, December, 16-17, 2010.

- Hames, Richard David. "Integral Systemic Foresight New Frontiers—New Challenges." Presentation at Foresight International Seminar: From Theory to Practice, sponsored by Centro de Gestao e Estudos Estrategicos (CGEE), Brasilia, Brazil, December, 16-17, 2010.

- Silberglitt, Richard. "Foresight in the local context." Presentation at Foresight International Seminar: From Theory to Practice, sponsored by Centro de Gestao e Estudos Estrategicos (CGEE), Brasilia, Brazil, December, 16-17, 2010.

- Ortega, Fernando. "Foresight Promotion In A Latin American Country: The Peruvian Case." Presentation at Foresight International Seminar: From Theory to Practice, sponsored by Centro de Gestao e Estudos Estrategicos (CGEE), Brasilia, Brazil, December, 16-17, 2010.

- Smith, Jack. "Building Resilience & Foresight Capacity: Framing Scenarios to Anticipate Disruption and Strategic Surprise." Presentation at Foresight International Seminar: From Theory to Practice, sponsored by Centro de Gestao e Estudos Estrategicos (CGEE), Brasilia, Brazil, December, 16-17, 2010.

- Johnston, Ron. "Foresight International Seminar." Presentation at Foresight International Seminar: From Theory to Practice, sponsored by Centro de Gestao e Estudos Estrategicos (CGEE), Brasilia, Brazil, December, 16-17, 2010.
- Cagnin, Cristiano. "Aspects to Consider when Designing Foresight Activities." Presentation at Foresight International Seminar: From Theory to Practice, sponsored by Centro de Gestao e Estudos Estrategicos (CGEE), Brasilia, Brazil, December, 16-17, 2010.
- Balaguer, Denis, L. "IT Systems and Technological Prospective: Some insights from Embraer's experience." Presentation at Foresight International Seminar: From Theory to Practice, sponsored by Centro de Gestao e Estudos Estrategicos (CGEE), Brasilia, Brazil, December, 16-17, 2010.
- Coelho, Gilda Massari "The application of information and knowledge management tools: Application of text mining in foresight studies." Presentation at Foresight International Seminar: From Theory to Practice, sponsored by Centro de Gestao e Estudos Estrategicos (CGEE), Brasilia, Brazil, December, 16-17, 2010.

[85] Porter, M.E. and Kramer, M.R. 2011. Creating shared value. Harvard Business Review, 89(1/2): 62-77.

[86] Cone, Carol. "2002 Cone Corporate Citizenship Study," Cone Communications.
Accessed February 6, 2012. http://www.coneinc.com/content1085

[87] Impacting The Community And The Bottom Line. Accessed march 2012. www.bsr.org

[88] Walsh, D.T. "Harness the Profit Motive to Deliver Environmental Sustainability," Huffington Post, November 5, 2010.
http://www.huffingtonpost.com/daniel-t-walsh/harness-the-profit-motive_b_779653.html

[89] Porter, M.E. and Kramer, M.R. 2011. Creating shared value. *Harvard Business Review*, 89(1/2): 62-77.

[90] Price Waterhouse Coopers. "CSR Trends 3," Craib Design & Communications, 2009.
http://www.pwc.com/ca/en/sustainability/publications/csr-trends-3-en.pdf

[91] Kenrick, Victoria. CEOs Embrace Sustainability. Environment Leader website. Accessed March 27, 2012. http://www.environmentalleader.com/2011/05/23/ceo's-embrace-sustainability/

92   Congressional Budget Office. "Trends in the Distribution of Household Income Between 1979 and 2007," October 2011. Accessed February 6, 2012. http://www.cbo.gov/doc.cfm?index=12485

93   Wikipedia. "Gini coefficient." Accesses February 6, 2012. http://en.wikipedia.org/wiki/Gini_coefficient

94   Weeks, J. Inequality Trends in Some Developed OECD countries. In J. K. S. & J. Baudot (Ed.), *Flat World, Big Gaps* (159-174). New York: ZED Books 2007.

95   Taft, Darryl, Cloud Computing: IBM's Top 12 Tech Trends for 2012, Accessed on March 21, 2012. http://www.eweek.com/c/a/Cloud-Computing/IBMs-Top-12-Tech-Trends-for-2012-Include-Cloud-Analytics-Mobile-221458/

INDEX